# The Art of Living

PHOTOGRAPHS BY BÄRBEL MIEBACH

TEXT BY CLAUDIA STEINBERG

# The Art of Living

THE MONACELLI PRESS

Copyright © 2009 by The Monacelli Press, a division of Random House, Inc.

Published in the United States by The Monacelli Press,
a division of Random House, Inc., New York.

The Monacelli Press and colophon are trademarks of Random House, Inc.

Library of Congress Cataloging-in-Publication Data
Miebach, Bärbel.
The art of living/photographs by Bärbel Miebach; text by Claudia Steinberg.—1st ed.
p. cm.
ISBN 978-1-58093-250-9 (hardcover)
1. Interior decoration—Themes, motives. I. Steinberg, Claudia. II. Title.
NK2113.M49 2009
747—dc22                    2009023995


Printed in China

10 9 8 7 6 5 4 3 2 1
First edition


Design by Susan Evans, *Design per se, Inc.*

www.monacellipress.com

# Contents

# Preface

As my ten-year anniversary of living and working in the United States approached, I began to feel nostalgic. I thought about the diverse, wonderful people I have photographed and the artistic environments they have built for themselves, and that became the spark of inspiration for this book.

*The Art of Living* introduces you to twenty-five unique homes; the book also tells twenty-five individual stories about their occupants. Artists, fashion designers, gallery owners, collectors, and one resourceful farmer express their personalities, idiosyncrasies, and creativity through their surroundings. I feel fortunate to have met them. They have inspired my own work and enriched my life.

I felt honored to spend a day with Ellsworth Kelly in Spencertown, New York. I learned so much about his work and his aesthetic. His partner prepared a delicious lunch, and we drank Ellsworth's favorite wine, Pouilly-Fuissé, while he reminisced about his time in Paris.

The fashion designer Catherine Malandrino was at the beginning of her career when I first met her and her husband, Bernard Aiden. At that time, I was fascinated by her eclectic mix of French bohemian elegance and urban New York chic, and to this day I continue to adore her.

Randolph Duke's house in the Hollywood hills with its breathtaking view of Los Angeles, its modern aesthetic, and unbelievably pleasant quality of life instantly became my dream home. When all the sliding glass doors were opened, I felt close to nature. While I was taking pictures I thought about how much I would love to live in a place like his.

Most surprising was my visit to the home of the artist Andres Serrano. His triplex in the West Village is filled with religious artifacts. Looking at the crucifixes, statues of saints, and pews all around me, I felt I had stepped into a medieval church in the center of Manhattan. It was an unsettling feeling that made me want to bring the photo shoot to an end quickly. When I returned for another shoot later, I came to understand the artist's personal reasons for having become such an obsessive collector. Today Andres Serrano is one of my best friends. I love him dearly.

I am profoundly grateful for the time I have spent in the U.S. and for the people I have met. They opened their homes to me and let me photograph their worlds. I cherish these experiences and hope to give you the same sense of wonder and admiration I felt when seeing these homes for the first time.

—Bärbel Miebach

# Souvenirs from a Full Life

Whenever this graceful nonagenarian strolls around New York, ambling through the farmer's market at Union Square or dropping into a Chelsea gallery, her majestic figure, crowned with a cap and dressed in long robes custom-made from exotic, precious fabrics, commands attention. Wide sleeves emphasize her expansive gestures, heavy bracelets clatter, huge rings flash on her slender fingers, and massive brooches and pendants arm her like shields against the ordinary. Ten Haeff's apartment on the north side of Washington Square, where she has lived since the middle of the twentieth century, reflects the same unique detailing as her wardrobe: precious accessories adorn every surface, whether wall, tabletop, or shelf.

Art is everywhere. There are works by her close friend Alfonso Ossorio, Joan Miró's painting *Woman, Bird, Sun*, and, in the center of the living room, a stabile by Alexander Calder that evokes the swarm its title, *Moths*, suggests. An abundance of souvenirs speak to a life lived across three continents, with three husbands, and the countless journeys taken. And ten Haeff's own abstract paintings share the scene. She came to art belatedly, having been trained as an actress and musician, but developed her own visual vocabulary rapidly in the 1950s after just a few courses at New York University. She was unsurprised by the quickness with which she developed this personal artistic language—she has studied Taoism her entire life, and believes that perfection exists in everyone from the very beginning, one only needs to recover it.

As the daughter of a well-known German industrialist, Ingeborg ten Haeff grew up in great wealth—the family's Berlin villa had forty-two rooms—and attended progressive schools and began moving in avant-garde circles. With her marriage to Dr. Lutero Vargas, the son of Brazil's president at the time, she fearlessly stepped onto the international stage—and found the boulevards of Rio de Janeiro very much to her liking. New York was a frequent destination during their travels together, and became her refuge when the marriage ended.

Ten Haeff's own painting receives pride of place above the mantel in the living room.

RIGHT: A sand-cast, cement sculpture by Costantino Nivola hangs to the left of the doorway, above an Amazon by surrealist sculptor Maria Martins.

OPPOSITE: Leather-and-steel dining chairs and a table designed by ten Haeff's second husband, architect Paul Lester Wiener sit in front of a Madonna, an antique candelabrum, and a painting by Kurt Seligmann.

In ten Haeff's floor-through apartment, it is Paul Lester Wiener, her second husband, who is still present in many ways. The Bauhaus-influenced architect and city planner designed the leather-and-steel chairs; the elegant wood-and-metal shelves now crowded with Japanese dolls, Korean boxes, and pre-Columbian vessels; and the long, slender coffee table with a bright red top. Soon after their wedding in 1948 the couple moved to Bogotá where Wiener, with his partner Josep Lluis Sert and Le Corbusier, developed a master plan for a city ravaged by civil unrest. Other projects led the couple to Peru, Venezuela, and Cuba. In these fabulous, itinerant years, ten Haeff became a connoisseur and collector of Latin American art. She eventually shipped her purchases north to share her home with her modern furniture and the single piece she had brought from Germany, a nineteenth-century candelabra once owned by her mother.

A few years after Wiener's death in 1966 ten Haeff married John Githens—a professor of Russian at Vassar College and a scholar of languages—and another chapter of far-flung travels began. They visited Japan, Korea, Taiwan, and Java for months at a time. Items found during those trips filled their suitcases, including fabrics—some of them so finely woven that they took a year to make—grand jewels, and humble stones picked from the ground or the water by ten Haeff "for their special mood, their very own temperament," she says. Today her personal version of Marcel Duchamp's legendary *Boîte-en-valise*, containing sixty-eight objects, is her favorite metaphor for her art-and-adventure-filled, nomadic life. Ten Haeff has felt at home all over the world because, she says, she always surrounded herself with the right people and with the right things.

LEFT: The main living space is graced with Joan Miró's painting *Woman, Bird, Sun,* at right; Paul Lester Wiener's passion scenes to its left; a work by ten Haeff's close friend Alfonso Ossorio, between the windows.

RIGHT: A view into the study of ten Haeff's husband, John Githens.

BELOW: A maquette by Nivola for Olivetti typewriters hangs above a stylized clothes hanger ten Haeff designed for Githens as a fiftieth birthday present.

RIGHT: Objects gathered while living on three different continents—including Japanese dolls, a red lacquer Korean box, and vessels from Latin America—rest on a 1932 étagère by Wiener.

OPPOSITE: Leather, chrome, and wood chairs, also by Wiener, blend gracefully with an eighteenth-century painting and a Moroccan rug.

FRANK FAULKNER

# Serving at the Altar of Art

Ever since he first transformed an old chicken coop on his parents' farm in North Carolina into a studio at the age of eight, Frank Faulkner has continued converting structures originally designed for other purposes into habitable spaces for his artistic pursuits. He has modified several industrial lofts in Soho and Chelsea and a carriage house in Greenwich Village, turning them into elegant dwellings filled with his collections of antique furniture, books, and paintings. He almost purchased what would have been his first "real" house— a Victorian—but on his way to sign the contract, he drove by two weathered churches, also for sale, that had been deconsecrated in 1996 for lack of attendance. Three months later, they were his. The sister sites give him a combined total of more than 10,000 square feet of living and studio space.

Furnishing the oversized rooms was easy for Faulkner. He had so many objects in storage that editing them down was more of a struggle than deciding how to fill the space; both structures were complete within three months. He allowed the proportions of the original architecture to guide the groupings of his eclectic possessions, using its restrained layout and disciplined composition to help him arrange his things so that they would not compete with each other or disrupt the otherwise serene space. "Classically arranged rooms will tell you how to move within them," he explains. Objects of different provenance and status are equally welcome in Faulkner's house. "A quarter century of finding, buying, and collecting has turned my household into a magnetic field where even the lost, the lonely, and the outsiders find a partner," he says. Fragments of rusty metal, primitive wooden tools, and faded upholstery are admitted as long as they reveal a similar symmetry and pureness of form as his fine Biedermeier tables, Regency chairs, and Art Deco fauteuils.

Faulkner approaches outfitting a house in the same way he maps a canvas: he follows his own sense of rhythm and structure to create layers of meaning. In his work, he builds up many coats of paint, then, when the surface is thick enough, carves a web of lines into it that creates a sort of relief. The neat, endless rows of freshly tilled soil that were part

Light from tall, paned windows floods the interior of this now-secular domestic space.

of his childhood still inspire him, and his affinity for Jasper Johns and Sol LeWitt's impeccable geometries are recognizable in his work as well. He admits that his eyes are constantly and almost obsessively drawn to patterns, grids, and parallel lines. His technique for the past thirty years has been to eschew the use of traditional easels, and to paint from a bird's-eye view instead, leaning over a canvas spread out on the ground, or on his thighs or knees in order to maintain an aerial perspective. He used his abilities with the brush in renovating his new space, too, in a synthesis of art and décor—one wall was painstakingly covered with marks that evoke the dots of a leopard or dappled feathers.

The larger of the two former churches serves as Faulkner's studio. He takes full advantage of its bold scale to lay out a dozen paintings at a time so that he can evaluate them from a distance. He formed an admiration for the building's mighty Corinthian columns instantly, but is taking longer to acquire a taste for the nave's more imposing architectural features: "I never liked stained glass windows, and neither organ music nor dark wainscoting please me. I never go to church. But eventually I will learn to love all this and serve at the altar of art. And the light falling through the colorful window is truly divine."

ABOVE, LEFT AND RIGHT: Formal, composed displays of Faulkner's many objects suit the classical architecture. The oversized Roman bust is a prop from the 1963 movie *Cleopatra*.

OPPOSITE: A long table divides and defines separate living areas in an otherwise wide open church hall. A niche is repurposed as a space for a daybed.

RIGHT: A fireplace and lamps made of artists' mannequins contribute to the cozy atmosphere in this sitting room. One of Faulkner's own paintings is displayed on the wall at right.

BELOW LEFT: Plenty of space allows Faulkner to exhibit arrangements of his antiques like this one, that includes urns, engravings, and a collection of antiquarian books.

BELOW RIGHT: Ample light encourages the display of art as well as its creation.

OPPOSITE: Views from a bedroom open onto the larger of the two church's stained glass windows, and a chair with a Gothic form references the ecclesiastical setting.

PREVIOUS PAGES: Antiques collected over a period of thirty years from high-end auction houses as well as local Hudson Valley flea markets fill the capacious church hall.

ABOVE: The nineteenth-century sanctuary with its Corinthian columns and stained glass windows, at right, was converted into an art studio. Faulkner chooses to live in the smaller building, the former church hall, at left.

OPPOSITE: Ample space in the sanctuary allows Faulkner to practice his technique of painting while standing directly over canvases positioned on the floor.

DAVID LING

# Serenity and Reflection

When this New York architect decided to create a home and office in a nineteenth-century structure, he permitted himself a luxury rarely afforded him by clients: time. He took the time to paint the back wall of the long ground floor with twenty-four layers of black, ultra-marine blue, and clear lacquer until it shone like enamel to reflect the shallow water basin at its base. Time to pour a six-ton block of black-pigmented concrete that would become a long kitchen counter and to sand it again and again until he was rewarded with a matte satin surface. He had to resist his own perfectionist tendencies in order to preserve visible signs of the building's 120-year-long history by reminding himself of the tenets of wabi-sabi, an aesthetic he became familiar with during several trips to Japan. The worldview prizes irregularities and even injuries that objects collect with use, and celebrates the beauty of transitoriness, instead of mourning the transitoriness of beauty.

Ling was also inspired by castle ruins along the Rhine he saw during his time as a student in Stuttgart. Using their ancient windows as models, he similarly eschewed frames and installed the glass from the outside. Existing skylights that had been covered with tar paper for decades were uncovered, and their light now reveals the building's old soul—weathered wooden beams, the roughness of whitewashed brick walls, and exposed heating pipes. These remnants contrast with the softly reflective modern silver floor that appears to be metal plate but is actually plastic, polished to a steely sheen.

Behind its typical Manhattan townhouse facade, the structure has always accommodated both working and living spaces: the downstairs was previously a denture factory and the small second story was also used as a bedroom during that time. Ling placed his office just beside the main entrance and hung semitransparent screens in front of a long row of

The bedroom cantilevers far out over an interior reflecting pool, filled with smooth river rocks, that separates working and living spaces. A fountain fitted to the underside of the second floor creates another visual division in the form of a wall of water.

RIGHT: The body of this torqued, conelike structure forms a seating area on the first floor and curves to become the bathroom wall upstairs.

OPPOSITE: Sun from the building's original skylights illuminates the bedroom and reflects off the metal surface.

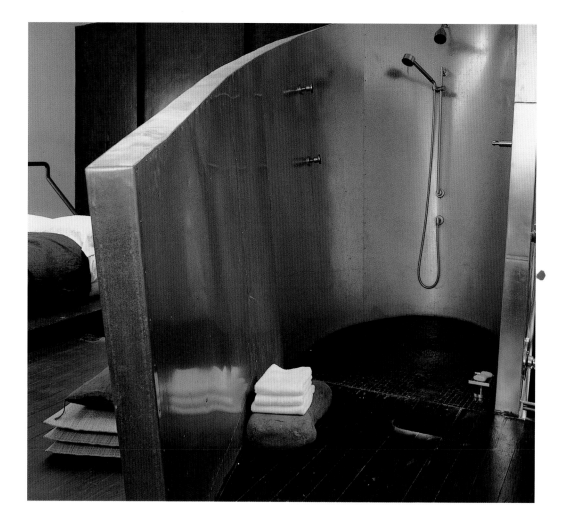

shelving to minimize visual distractions and clutter. To indicate a private place in the back for lounging, reading, and eating while keeping an open sightline through the generous expanse, he created symbolic walls of light and water. A moat separates the office area from the living space, spanned by a bridge of rough wooden planks. The wide avenue that extends through the office ends at a second body of water, a shallow reflecting pool.

A prominent zinc sculpture hovers over this feature, functioning as a kind of throne, complete with a luxuriously lined seat of silver fox fur. At its top, the curved shell opens wide and, with one sweeping gesture, transforms into the second-floor bathroom wall. Downstairs, serenity may rule, but on the second floor the balance tips toward a rather risky arrangement: with the bed on a cantilevered platform veering into open space like a springboard, Ling rejects the sense of safety one instinctively craves during sleep, when we are at our most vulnerable. Perhaps sleeping on the edge of an abyss is the perfect counterweight to living and working in an otherwise tranquil, Zen atmosphere.

The brilliant violet-blue color of the far wall was inspired by Yves Klein and created by applying twenty-four layers of black, ultramarine, and clear lacquer to the original brick wall. While the floor appears to be metal, it is actually plastic, polished to a high sheen.

LEFT: A broad avenue through the office is flanked by a row of three low wooden pedestals, covered with tatami mats, that serve as dining tables and also occasionally as guest beds. The six-ton block of black concrete that forms the kitchen counter stands prominently at right.

TOP: A view over the moat that separates office and living spaces, toward the reflecting pool.

ABOVE: Semitransparent screens line a wall of shelves in the office, minimizing visual clutter and extending the tranquil atmosphere.

JEANNE GREENBERG ROHATYN

# Effortless Elegance

Gallery owner Jeanne Greenberg Rohatyn lives near New York's Museum Mile in a four-story, Parisian-style townhouse occupying not one, but two, city lots, bought to accommodate her understandably superb art collection. In her words, she seeks out paintings and sculptures that can be deemed nervous, unsettling, or aggressive to provide her a daily dose of subversive beauty and intellectual stimulation. David Hammons's basketball hoop adorned with the crystal tears of a chandelier hanging in a hallway fits the concept, as do Kara Walker's life-sized silhouettes depicting surreal, cruel, and perverse scenes from the antebellum South in an old-fashioned medium.

This building—the former headquarters of the Louise Wise Adoption Agency, known for rescuing many Jewish children from Europe during World War II—appealed to her because of its extremely high ceilings. After completely gutting the townhouse, she and her husband Nicholas Rohatyn hired Rafael Viñoly to transform its fin-de-siècle shell into a home with maximum space devoted to the display of art. Especially low fireplaces were designed so as not to encroach on the vast walls. The art, which is often informed by classical ideals of beauty but then fragmented or defaced in a postmodern way, blurs the distinction between gallery and domestic space. The whole evokes the adventurous spirit of earlier female collectors and patrons like Gertrude Stein, Peggy Guggenheim, and Florine Stettheimer, whose avant-garde salons were a source of inspiration.

With the grand spiral staircase, Viñoly introduced the house's most opulent, baroque element. He conceived the complex Art Nouveau curve of the polished, burled walnut railing with the aid of a computer, and it blends perfectly with the French aesthetic developed in the living room, where two parenthesis-shaped Napoleonic sofas sit among a mix of pieces from the early 1930s and 1940s. The couple eliminated as possible distractions from the art all of the moldings, ornate doorknobs, and curtain rods. In general, the furniture—including a few flea market finds—is kept comparatively modest to keep the focus on the collection.

Chiho Aoshima's mural *Mountain Girls*, 2003, a sculpture by Huma Bhabha, and a red chair by Martino Gamper keep company with a French sofa in the living room.

ABOVE: Wardell Milan's collage series *Battle Royale*, 2007, is displayed on the curving stairwell, and a Pae White chandelier hangs in front of a Marilyn Minter piece.

OPPOSITE: Chris Ofili's *Blue Rider* anchors the far end of the living room. Two Diego Giacometti chairs sit in front of a custom coffee table that holds a varied collection of small objects.

Rohatyn explains that her relative indifference to decorative objects stems from the Spartan environment she experienced as a child in St. Louis. Her mother, an art-book author, and her father, an art dealer, were decided minimalists and opted for an extremely reduced yet highly aestheticized life. Out of exasperation, her mother finally bought a couch one day, but the young Jeanne had already gotten used to the concept of art paired with emptiness. The exquisite bronze chairs Diego Giacometti had given her father as a gift to thank him for arranging one of his first U.S. exhibitions were only taken out of the basement in the summer as garden furniture. Although her father passed them on to her as a present, so far she still hasn't developed a close relationship to these treasures. "I will learn to love them," she promises. After all, they are works of art in their own right, if only terribly useful.

LEFT: Two Takashi Murakami daisies, a Julie Mehretu painting, and the far left section of Chiho Aoshima's mural form a colorful ensemble at one end of the living room.

RIGHT: A graceful curve of the Rafael Viñoly–designed burled walnut staircase.

BELOW: Blue, green, and purple colors on this lamp pop against the black background of a painting with a recurring motif of abstract shapes.

TOP: Malerie Marder's *The Marder Sisters*, 2000, watch over a guest room done in shades of red.

ABOVE: Art also finds a place in the kitchen—a Mika Kato painting hangs over the banquette at left.

RIGHT: Life-sized Kara Walker silhouettes and Wangechi Mutu's *The Mare*, 2007, are large-scale additions to the dining area. A Paula Hayes terrarium occupies the table.

ELLSWORTH KELLY

# Playful Geometry

When Ellsworth Kelly first presented his flatly painted, unsigned canvases to the public in the early 1950s, their stunning emptiness came as a shock. Undeterred, he has continued producing sculptures and monochromatic works in strong, unique, geometric shapes that demand space to express their bold personalities. The artist considers each of his works to be its own person, to possess its own identity. In his paintings, each color or form receives its own territory, but he recognizes that each is also inevitably influenced by its neighbor. When they escape the familiar rectangular shape so traditionally used for paintings and tilt, overlap each other, or form idiosyncratic shapes instead, they become sculptural objects in their own right.

Like his creations, Ellsworth Kelly also requires open expanses for full self-expression: in 1970 he left New York City, where he had been part of an artistic community that included Robert Rauschenberg, Jasper Johns, and Agnes Martin, for quiet Spencertown in upstate New York. In 2005, craving even more space for creative pursuits, he expanded his existing studio to 17,500 square feet with the help of architect Richard Gluckman. His work still spills over into his house, however—he has installed two permanent sculptures made of painted aluminum in the entry hall, one placed directly inside the front door, the other bordering an interior passageway. Together they exude a powerful aura unexpected in this otherwise traditional 1920s country house. Clearly, no other objects are needed or wanted in their vicinity.

Other rooms under the copper roof, however, harbor a multitude of objects from far away places and times. The fireplace mantle in the dining room, for example, holds an array of elegant weapons from Melanesia and Polynesia, an African reliquary figure, a small Georges Braque landscape, an American Indian ceremonial copper shield, and a meteorite from a crater in Arizona. A 1,300-year-old Buddha sits on the dining table while behind it hangs an Antoni Gaudí mirror, its highly ornate frame a surprising presence in an environment domi-nated by stark and simple shapes, like the neat stack of oval Shaker boxes or Gerrit Rietveld's still-radical ZigZag chair. A collection of bannerstones serves as an endless source of inspira-tion: no matter how platonically pure Kelly's paintings may appear on a museum wall, they are firmly rooted in shapes and objects drawn from reality. "My paintings are fragments of the world," he says, "I'm simply digging them up and presenting them."

Two of the artist's geometric sculptures installed in the front hall, *White Ring*, 1963, and *White Curves*, 1978, redefine conven-tional notions of doorways.

ABOVE: A simple collection of Shaker boxes from the mid-1800s in various oval shapes and sizes rest on the shelves while a square Northwest Coast Indian drum from the nineteenth century hangs on the wall.

RIGHT: A fighting club from the Solomon Islands, far left, is arranged with a Georges Braque landscape painting, a Kota tomb figure from Gabon at center, a meteorite, a Northwest Coast Indian ceremonial copper shield, and a war club from Tonga.

ABOVE: Kelly's collection of 4,000-year-old Native American bannerstones.

LEFT: An eighth century figure of Buddha from central Java watches over a rustic table set for guests, an Antoni Gaudí Calvet mirror hangs on the rear wall.

A simply appointed living space allows the eye to rest on primitive art, artifacts, and art books. A ceremonial Northwest Coast copper hangs, centered, behind the circa 1850 Shaker table, and an early-twentieth-century Zulu container sits on the table in the foreground.

ANDREA ZITTEL

# Artistry in the High Desert

With its ruined houses, empty shacks, abandoned mines, and military bases, the Mojave Desert has haunted artist Andrea Zittel since she first photographed it as a student in the early 1980s. Twenty years later, after designing and living for several months on a self-contained, 44-ton fiberglass-and-cement island anchored off the shore of Denmark that drew more attention from curious spectators than she had anticipated, she began to search the Internet for a remote refuge in this lonesome California landscape. The modest 1930s house she found near Joshua Tree National Park seemed perfect for the pursuit of a life focused on living with only the bare necessities, an ongoing theme at the core of her work. After her own aborted experiment in the Baltic Sea, she felt drawn to the melancholic relics of broken dreams and failed Utopias littering the Mojave Desert. Most of these settlements were initiated by the ratification of the Small Tract Act of 1938, which gave five acres to anyone willing to try and improve the inhospitable land; few attempts were successful and most have been long since abandoned.

Zittel describes the homestead cabin she found at the foot of a rounded mountain as "rather unique, because someone renovated it in the sixties and turned it into a modernist building with a Palm Springs feel to it." The interior walls had suffered severe water damage, however, and urgently needed a cover-up. Always drawn to affordable materials, Zittel opted for generic birch plywood, an inexpensive solution that creates a sleek, modern look. Her large-scale furniture pieces appear to be boulders, but are actually carved slabs of charcoal-gray foam. This single material is used to form the desk, coffee table, and sofa, and Zittel always has a knife handy to reshape these artificial stone formations for new needs, or to swiftly cut off an accidentally damaged corner.

The exterior of Zittel's modest 1930s homestead house.

ABOVE: A desk carved from a single block of foam.

ABOVE RIGHT: The bedspread and wall hanging are two examples of Zittel's fiber art.

OPPOSITE: Zittel's A-Z Raugh Uniforms—clothing made from raw, felted wool intended to be the primary garment worn each day for an entire season.

Her well-organized kitchen was custom-built in Northern California according to Zittel's instructions and shipped whole to Joshua Tree. She finds cooking boring and lonely, so here meals are prepared on a grill set directly into the small dining table, and the act becomes a cooperative enterprise. In her quest to live with bare essentials only, Zittel also eliminated plates by carving two slightly amorphous indentations directly into the table's thick plywood top, revealing layers that evoke the elevation lines on a topographical map.

Zittel achieved international recognition in the 1990s for her Escape Vehicles, streamlined, freestanding silver capsules that reference the American camper tradition and can be customized to provide a tailor-made retreat for one individual owner. In 2003, she began constructing similar A-Z Wagon Stations, inspired by the covered wagons used by original pioneers. Much of her Arte Povera centers around explorations of the domestic sphere, so it is only fitting that she creates most of her art at home in the desert—including the abstract knitted, crocheted, and hand knotted shapes that form garments produced by her tongue-in-cheek A-Z Administrative Services company. These elevate low-tech needlework and low-status materials to a progressive art form aimed at stretching limited resources—Zittel wears one of these versatile dresses for six months straight, an entire fashion season.

Originally Zittel believed that her five-acre desert property would facilitate the production of large-scale works, but she soon found that the climate dictated its own terms. Several of the metal pods she had placed around the grounds were ripped apart and smashed against stones by the choleric wind, and she had to redesign them to be more aerodynamically resilient. In spite of her vulnerabilities in this hostile environment, Zittel persists in using the rocky site as a laboratory for developing new materials, like recycled paper pulp baked into marblelike blocks by the sun. She has assembled a studio from three white shipping containers for storage, tools, and her larger projects, and their horseshoe configuration surrounds a patio planted with orderly rows of mesquite trees, forming a personal oasis.

Zittel at work in her modest living room. The birch paneling covering the ceiling was an inexpensive fix for the irregular, damaged surface, yet conveys a modern feeling.

LEFT: Unique, custom-built kitchen furniture designed to maximize storage and make the act of cooking a collaborative rather than solitary process.

RIGHT: The only cooking surface, a simple grill, is built directly into the tabletop, as are the recessed 'dishes.'

BELOW: Zittel updated the original bathroom herself with simple square tiles and more birch cabinetry.

RIGHT, BELOW, AND OPPOSITE:
Examples of A-Z Wagon Stations,
portable pods intended to be
customized by their owners.
Zittel's A-Z West property reveals
how her land has become both a
showroom and a testing ground
for her work.

OVERLEAF: Three shipping
containers form Zittel's studio.

KATHLEEN TRIEM AND PETER FRANCK

# Light Glides Through a Copper Shell

New York City is more than a hundred miles away yet always present in this upstate house. Kathleen Triem and Peter Franck were ready to move to the country, but after decades spent in city spaces, could not envision living in a quaint nineteenth-century house with portly furniture and a garden with rosebushes. Together, the pair of architects designed a contemporary structure with high ceilings and white walls that recall a Soho loft, and a broad, segmented window inspired by Chelsea galleries. "I still have one foot in Manhattan," says Franck. Their former view of brick-and-mortar canyons, however, has been replaced with the gentle undulations of the Catskill Mountains.

Triem was invited to plan and curate a new sculpture garden at Art Omi, a residency program for painters, writers, and musicians in Ghent, New York, in 1996, an opportunity she couldn't miss. Franck soon followed her upstate, they married, and shared Art Omi's existing villa with visiting artists from around the world. After three years of communal life, they bought a neighboring piece of farmland on which to build a house of their own. With the help of a tall ladder, they determined how high their future house would have to be in order to provide views over the treetops to the grand Catskill panorama beyond. They even camped in a tent on the property for an entire summer in order to get to know it intimately before deciding how to site the structure.

Growing up in Chicago, Franck studied Frank Lloyd Wright's residences and their sensitive relationship between architecture and nature, and sought to re-create that delicate balance here. "We wanted the house to appear as a minimalist object that surprises from every angle," explains Triem. They decided on a trapezoidal shape, which exposes its 14-foot-high,

A loftlike, open room contains Lucite tables and wooden chairs designed by Triem and Franck.

ABOVE: A chaise longue placed next to the master bedroom's window receives warming rays from the unfiltered sunlight.

ABOVE RIGHT: A sculpture of branches and layers of paper by Steven Siegel.

OPPOSITE: Art by Triem fills this sitting room: a series of three drawings hangs on the wall at left, and a collage made primarily of photographs is displayed on a backlit Duratrans film.

wide window front to the Hudson Valley and tapers to half that height at the opposite end. The square footage provided by this largely open-plan volume totals 3,000 square feet and comprises living, dining, and kitchen spaces on the upper level, and on the lower level, a playroom for the couple's children and a painting and photography studio for Triem.

Creating the appearance of a homogenous, geometric volume that was as much a sculpture in the landscape as the pieces of art around it was so important to the couple that they perforated the side facades with only a few rather small openings. Two slender wooden ramps give access to the building like gangways and add an unexpected element of grace to this hull-like structure. The notion of cladding the building in a metal shell was inspired by a copper sculpture in the nearby park that glowed like a lantern in the afternoon light. Even before construction of their house was complete, the copper had begun to lose its reddish shine and oxidize into a dark matte armor. They could have sealed it against verdigris, but decided against it. "At some point," says Franck enthusiastically, "it will be green like the Statue of Liberty."

LEFT: White surfaces, a terrazzo floor and industrial windows recall a Soho loft.

RIGHT: The couple's children relax in a bedroom injected with a shot of vibrant color.

BELOW: Mirrored tiles surrounding the fireplace continue the play of light throughout the interior.

LEFT: A sculpture from the adjacent Art Omi Fields Sculpture Park by Philip Grausman.

BELOW: Copper cladding encases the house; small windows on opposite sides provide cross-ventilation to keep it naturally cool.

RIGHT: Position, layout, and the house's trapezoidal shape were determined by views; the local bluestone foundation was chosen for its rough surface, which provides a textural contrast to the smooth copper above.

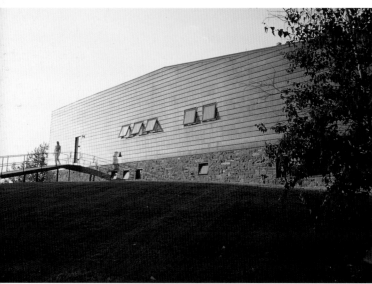

KATHLEEN TRIEM AND PETER FRANCK

PAUL DISCOE AND ANN HATCH

# A Japanese Farmhouse in Manhattan

First, a subtle, spicy fragrance, not incense, but a scent emanating from the five kinds of wood —elm, fir, camphor tree, cedar, and pine—used for the floors, ceilings, walls and furniture. Then, an unusual quiet as visitors take off their shoes and step onto the elevated floor covered with simple tatami mats: voices intuitively fall to a whisper. And finally, a surprise for the eyes as they take in what appears to be a traditional Japanese farmhouse right in Manhattan, complete with an *engawa*, normally an exterior walkway providing access to each room from the outside. In this city incarnation, it runs parallel with the building's exterior wall, along a row of tall, paned windows. This long, serene hall unites four airy rooms separated by sliding shoji screens. Each element of the urban refuge was designed to gently soothe, instilling a calm the owners cherish.

With this at once utterly simple and highly sophisticated home, Paul Discoe—an ordained Soto Zen priest—re-created a house he occupied while learning the art of temple building during an intensive five-year program under a master builder in Japan in the 1980s, where he was advised to go by his mentor, Suzuki Roshi of the Tassajara Zen Mountain Center in northern California. He has since applied this hard-won skill to the construction of temples and residences, and most important, a weekend house near San Francisco for the art collector, educator, and philanthropist Ann Hatch, an enthusiastic client who eventually became his wife.

In his downtown oasis, this native Californian now finds peace. As a child in Berkeley, he was intrigued by the orderly manners of the Japanese neighbors across the street and subsequently became fascinated with Japanese culture in general. However, it took a souvenir from the West Coast to make him feel at home here: five blue basalt rocks harvested from the Yuba River in the Sierra Nevada Mountains were expertly, precisely placed in the sunken, pebble-lined indoor garden by master rock setter Shigeru Namba to create energy between them. When guests are expected, water is poured over the stones to bring out their character and to make them shine.

Shoji screens and an indoor meditation garden create a Zen mood unexpected in a city apartment.

ABOVE, LEFT AND RIGHT: An *engawa*, or walkway, runs the length of the apartment and connects its various rooms; an art installation by Tony Feher, in the window, overlooks Cooper Square.

OPPOSITE, ABOVE: Tatami mats surround a table in a recess; the low sight line achieved when sitting in the chairs is meant to quell feelings of stress or aggression.

OPPOSITE, BELOW: The entry reveals elements of Discoe's building philosophy and exacting standards: the post is a reclaimed city tree, and the tiles were set without the use of grout.

It took several years of meticulous planning before the couple embarked on the transformation of their large, almost empty loft. The complexities of New York building codes kept delaying the process—so unexpected was this exotic undertaking that officials at the city's building department, misreading Discoe's drawings of shoji grids for brick walls, attempted to require him to install specially fortified floors for what would actually be almost weightless architecture. Discoe drew on his training and the Zen attention to mindfulness and technique when laying the tiles of the kitchen floor as well. He banned grout, calling for the tiles to be placed with an almost unheard-of exactitude instead.

The first in the suite of four open rooms contains only a small table placed with a base rising out of a square recess, and four surrounding, legless chairs. Following the Zen tenet of making do with what's at hand, Paul Discoe built other pieces of furniture in the apartment from shipping crates their few store-bought items arrived in.

A love of trees originally brought Discoe and Hatch together—she inherited a large forest, and wanted to construct the house she hired Discoe to build with timber from her own land. Some of this was also fitted into the Manhattan space, but as a matter of principle Discoe mainly works with lumber from what he calls "the urban forest," city trees felled by cars, removed from construction sites, or killed by vandals. "When trees live around people, they incorporate the history of cohabitation—nails, ropes, even bullets leave their traces and become part of their unique personality," says Discoe. He strongly believes that the karmic energy of exquisite workmanship can ennoble even the scraggliest street tree, making it fit to be turned into fine furniture.

RIGHT: A view through the bedroom; the nightstand is created from packaging other furniture arrived in, an example of the Zen tenet of making do with materials on hand.

OPPOSITE: Cushion seating surrounding a low table clearly reveals Japanese influence.

OVERLEAF: Five blue basalt rocks shipped from Discoe's native California were placed by master rock setter Shigeru Namba.

LEFT: Tiles in the kitchen give a bright splash of color to a space filled with otherwise muted tones.

RIGHT: Woods used on the interior are left in natural colors to evoke nature.

BELOW: A unique towel rack designed by Discoe is a decorative but functional addition to an otherwise minimalist bathroom.

MICHAEL HALL

# Life in a Treasure Chest

This obsessive collector is always struggling to create the illusion of space in his townhouse near the Metropolitan Museum of Art in New York, employing what he dubs "room stretchers," like the occasional mirror or bare surface. When he realized that this house was two feet wider than his previous brownstone, he temporarily felt space-rich enough to establish a rule: each piece of furniture should have a six-inch aura of emptiness around it. The never-ending flow of objects flooding his four-story home, however, soon led him to abandon this ambition, and he now admits that his treasures are actually touching each other—and even, he suspects, multiplying. "You need pathways," he acknowledges. But this clutter that Hall has amassed from the age of ten is of the highest order: tapestries woven for Catherine de Medici, marble busts of kings and queens, African figures wearing opulent coral jewelry, and a baroque Portuguese settee. His Canaletto depicting gondolas and the campanile of St. Mark's Basilica he casually calls "a postcard from Venice," his favorite place in the world.

It was his grandmother who inspired his passion for collecting. In 1933 she took him to the opening of the art museum in his hometown of Kansas City, where he was fascinated by della Robbia terra cotta roundels made in the fifteenth and sixteenth centuries. Hall now calls several his own. A year later, grandmother and grandson attended the World's Fair in Chicago. To this day, he remembers the excitement he felt at visiting the Asian pavilions— they revealed a whole new continent full of treasures.

At twenty Hall appeared in a small role in William Wyler's Oscar-winning masterpiece *The Best Years of Our Lives*. About 250 movies, most for early television, and a glamorous life in Hollywood followed. Then, after fifteen years in the film industry and several Broadway appearances, Hall exchanged what he calls a second-rate acting career for the life of a first-rate art collector and dealer. To his mind nothing compares to the experience of "learning by buying"—inspecting, caressing, and living with an exquisite piece of art.

In a fantastically appointed sitting room, an eighteenth-century parasol that shaded the doge of Venice keeps company with an Egypto-Roman drilled basalt bust of Antinous on the stair landing; one of Hall's own gouaches in blue above; a silk Isfahan rug shot through with gold threads, from the late seventeenth century, on the wall; and a pair of Fa-hua garden seats from the Ming dynasty.

How to create harmony among Chinese vases, Oriental rugs, statues of the Buddha, grand chandeliers, a fountain with Hercules as an infant holding a water-spewing snake, and a John Singer Sargent oil study is a question Hall keeps pondering. In the end, he just relies on his theory that all beautiful things belong together, as long as they fit the two important aesthetic categories he recognizes: the grotesque or the sublime.

There are many examples of the former in his house, like the ugly, witty, and exquisitely carved marble masks by Michelangelo's protégé Niccolò Tribolo that hang on his dining room walls. Hall sees the sublime in the figure of a seated Bodhisattva with one leg crossed and the other draped over its pedestal. And he savored the sublime pleasure of discovering several Bernard Palissy plates that feature flamboyant, high-relief creatures. Hall is proud of such finds and his self-trained discerning eye: "You are born with taste," he believes, "but you can teach yourself to become a connoisseur." Ideally by owning the fine things you have learned to love.

ABOVE: In the dining room, a seventeenth-century mirror frame from Bologna is flanked by a collection of maiolica plaques by Bernard Palissy from the sixteenth century, which are in turn set off by two busts by the fifteenth-century Florentine Nanni di Banco.

ABOVE RIGHT: One of Hall's earliest purchases, at the age of twenty: a seventeenth-century Venetian sculpture of an African in a turban. The coral jewelry and feather headdress were added later, by Hall.

OPPOSITE: A large Canaletto depicting the doge's pleasure boat, or *bucintoro*, presides over the living room. Eighteenth-century French bronze sconces adorn the wall beneath it and a French seventeenth-century sculpture of Ariadne lounges on a green porphyry tabletop.

LEFT: A seventeenth-century mirror made by Venetian craftsmen features etched glass and églomisé panels with a blue glass overlay—it is the only item from Hall's family estate in the house. An Italian seventeenth-century lapis lazuli orb on a jasper column sits in front.

BELOW: An English mirror of Vauxhall glass hangs above a mantel that holds a pair of Ming Fa-hua jars, Italianate candlesticks from the mid-eighteenth century, and a Meissen clock with a whimsical monkey figurine. A Roman statue depicting a rare female satyr stands below.

RIGHT: A nineteenth-century Tibetan rug anchors a room filled with elm Bodhisattvas, upper right; a graphite portrait of Ethel Barrymore—one of Hall's good friends—on the far right; his collection of minerals, on the table; and a pair of glove leather chairs by Emile-Jacques Ruhlmann with maple frames and an inlay of mahogany. A roundel by Bernini sits just above the left-hand chair's top edge, and a portrait of that artist hangs directly above it.

LEFT: With a real ruby on her forehead, a rare unbaked Bodhisattva watches over a late-seventeenth-century Spanish bench with a yellow cushion; a table with a top of an unusually large piece of petrified wood—the other half of which is at the Smithsonian; a Venini glass side table; and an early Ming bowl, left rear.

RIGHT: A seventeenth-century Dutch desk with gold chinoiserie detailing holds a collection of mirror black vases, a baked clay bust from China, and a collection of eighteenth-century continental porcelain figurines. Shelves on the wall at right are formed of papier-mâché and can fold completely flat. A Meissen dog guards the group.

BELOW: Ming chairs, circa 1500, are flanked by eighteenth-century Venetian tables painted with red lacquer.

VIVIENNE TAM

# An Alchemy of Tender and Tough

The careful mix of materials in this north Greenwich Village apartment is alchemy: a bit of the precious in milk-white porcelain and a dose of the brutal in stark concrete columns melt almost magically into quiet minimalism. "I wanted my home to resemble a traditional Chinese garden, celebrating every aspect of nature: earth as much as blossoms, roots and stones no less than trees and flowering bushes," says fashion designer Vivienne Tam. She grew up in Hong Kong, where living, evolving gardens are designed to balance the static nature of a house. Tam interpreted this custom for her city apartment; she has removed most of the interior walls, stripped off Sheetrock to expose the 1970s building's concrete bones, and eliminated nonessential doors in order to create unobstructed paths through a varying landscape of rough and smooth surfaces. Elements of her upbringing taught Tam to harmonize contradictory concepts: she dressed like a boy but kept a feminine haircut, she attended Catholic school—and sewed her own uniforms—while practicing Buddhism.

Now, as the head of her eponymous fashion house known for its sophisticated, China Chic fusion of traditional Asian textiles and styles with what she calls "Europeanoiserie," Tam urgently needs this center of peace and quiet. When she embarked on renovations with designer Scott Crolla—responsible for the exquisite finishes—she also consulted a feng shui master, who approved of the apartment's southern orientation, but told her that the light and energy surging against the building's large plate glass windows could never be stilled, not even with her introduction of uncluttered planes, large islands of empty space, and the palette of natural colors with its touches of crimson, notably on the lacquered front door.

A wall finished in a subtle silver reflects soft light deep into the interior.

And yet, she appears to have succeeded. Silence seems to emanate from the matte shimmer of walls polished to look like mother-of-pearl and the white-on-white Robert Ryman painting above the limestone fireplace. Throughout her home, Tam has tried to evoke "a very Ming feeling" that she describes as a balance of sun and moon to create luminosity and clarity. The dynasty ruled peacefully, and she believes that calm is reflected in furniture from its era.

Tam has roamed the antique stores of Hong Kong's famous Hollywood Road in search of chairs and tables of that period. An expert even taught her how to verify a piece's age by tapping it and listening to the vibration. As a young girl, she slept on a bed made of wide slats covered with bamboo matting; in her sparsely appointed meditation room, she can recline on a Ming bed reminiscent of her childhood. Normally, the many souls who have slept on the 400-year-old piece of furniture would disturb her rest, she believes, but the feng shui master reassured her: ghosts can't cross the ocean.

ABOVE LEFT: Light filters through wooden blinds onto a Ming bed.

ABOVE RIGHT: Robert Ryman's white-on-white painting adds dimension without disturbing the visual calmness of the living room's neutral palette.

OPPOSITE: Milky porcelain figures from Tam's homeland contribute to the Chinese theme.

In the living room, Ming Dynasty chairs and a Scandinavian coffee table prove that the modern can coexist calmly with the old.

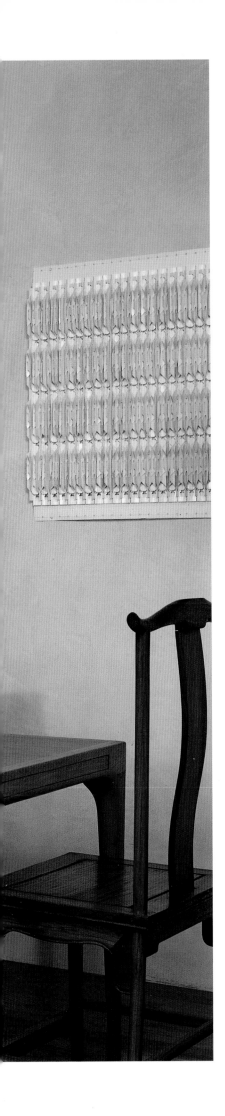

LEFT: Dining room furniture continues the mix of contemporary and antique found throughout Tam's home.

RIGHT: An art piece featuring a silhouette of Chairman Mao provides one of the apartment's hits of traditional Chinese red.

BELOW: Structural concrete columns were exposed and given alternating rough and smooth finishes.

FAR LEFT: A Chinese scholar's rock resting on a demilune table echoes the roughly hewn surface of the apartment's columns nearby.

LEFT: An intricately carved Buddha placed in front of paneled art features a pattern of flowers and foliage like those often found on Tam's garments.

BELOW: Marbles of three different colors and textures combine in the master bath.

OPPOSITE: A stylized Chinese garment hangs in the bedroom, referencing Tam's profession and adding another layer of shine to the interior.

RUTH NIVOLA

# The Past is Perfect

"Your house is marvelous," exclaimed Le Corbusier when he visited Ruth and Costantino Nivola in Amagansett, New York, in 1950, "but it urgently needs a mural." Nivola, a Sardinian sculptor and painter fetched brushes and paint, and his mentor—who at the time was also occupied with the design for the United Nations—immediately set to work. In just a few days, his semiabstract fresco became the new heart of the 1754 farmhouse, and even sixty years later it pounds with undiminished vitality. This enigmatic composition is hardly the only modern artwork to find an unexpected home in these modest rooms: there is a Josef Albers in the living room, an Alexander Calder mobile in the foyer, and, in the staircase, Saul Steinberg's portrait of one of the Nivolas' dogs, fashioned from precisely torn pieces of a simple brown paper bag. But most ubiquitous are Costantino's paintings, sculptures, ceramics, and furniture.

In the 1930s, when Ruth enrolled in a Bauhaus-based art school in Monza, after immigrating to Italy from Frankfurt during Hitler's rise to power, she was assigned a drawing table next to Costantino's. It sat empty for the first several months of her attendance, however, because he had been temporarily suspended for refusing to perform the fascist salute, and during that time her curiosity about him grew. They eventually met and married, in 1938, and briefly became involved with the Italian resistance, but fled to New York shortly before the outbreak of World War II, taking refuge in a small Greenwich Village apartment. By day, Ruth worked in a textile factory and Costantino drew ads for the department store Bonwit Teller, but in the evenings they hosted other European émigrés and scores of artists and architects, including Isamu Noguchi, Willem de Kooning, and Marcel Breuer.

A mural painted spontaneously by Le Corbusier and one of Costantino Nivola's sculptures are unexpected decorations for this farmhouse room.

ABOVE, LEFT AND RIGHT: The somber, weighty presence of the nineteenth-century stove—still in use—is countered by brightly colored pots, a lacquered red rocking chair, and a bright yellow floor.

OPPOSITE, ABOVE: Unique modern shelving designed by Costantino Nivola, at right, references traditional screened-in food storage from the days before refrigeration.

OPPOSITE, BELOW: While the rest of the house is filled with art, the kitchen is decorated with baskets from Costantino Nivola's hometown in Sardinia.

When the Nivolas decided to move to Amagansett in the late 1940s—then a very rural area—they found this Colonial-style farmhouse at the end of a long, winding road. They were instantly charmed by the house—and undaunted by its weathered condition and its fifteen acres of unkempt grounds. A son of bitterly poor stonemasons, Costantino had grown up accustomed to backbreaking labor, and enthusiastically devoted himself to the house's renovation. "Tino did everything with his own hands—he built the low living room table and covered its top with black linoleum, he made the bookshelves and the bench in the kitchen," reminisced Ruth. "He even recycled the children's old toys into lamps." Floors and walls were painted in bright, primary colors, and a round, fragrant carpet of lilies of the valley was planted in the garden.

The beach is less than a mile away, and while playing there with his children Costantino developed his famous technique of casting plaster and cement reliefs in sand. He eventually built a studio in the garden and painted the walls the azure of the Sardinian sky. Countless marble, plaster, and black bronze sculptures—based on prehistoric clay figures from his homeland—lend the crowded space and grounds, which are peppered with his own stone sculptures, the appearance of a rich archaeological site.

Despite the numerous works of art that fill the house and yard, it maintains a richly hospitable atmosphere—the rooms' joyous colors, painted so long ago, are still fresh and intense. The spirit and passion of the many modernist artists and luminaries who visited throughout the years have been perfectly preserved here, as if in a time capsule. Objects that would elsewhere be displayed behind glass were here lived with, like friends, for the whole of Ruth's lifetime.

LEFT: Several of the farmhouse's internal walls were removed to open the space and better display the works created by the couple's many artistic friends, including Josef Albers, whose bright yellow study painting of nesting squares hangs on the wall at left.

RIGHT: Family photographs and an Italian newspaper hint at the couple's earlier years in Europe.

BELOW: An arrangement of small sculptures, including three of Nivola's own at right, add presence to a low bookshelf in the living room.

A full view of Le Corbusier's 1950 mural, spontaneously created upon his first visit to the Nivolas' house with paints that were on hand.

LEFT: Every surface in the house holds some form of art, including this bedroom windowsill.

BELOW: Saul Steinberg's portrait of the Nivolas' dog rendered in bits of brown paper bag watches over the stairwell.

OPPOSITE: Simple furnishings and textiles are accompanied by art from the Nivolas' many friends in this guest bedroom.

LEFT: Nivola's sculptures are placed in groupings throughout the yard.

BELOW: The studio's walls are painted in an azure blue meant to evoke the color of Costantino Nivola's native Sardinian sky.

RIGHT: Sculptures and photographs in the studio are still placed much as Costantino Nivola left them.

RANDOLPH DUKE

# Into the Open

A simple hunch that something interesting might be hidden behind an iron gate on a site for sale high in the Hollywood hills prompted fashion designer Randolph Duke to call his realtor. Duke was the first one through during the open house the next morning, and found that his intuition had been right. Panoramic views of Los Angeles unfolded at his feet, prompting him to immediately declare it the best—and only—possible location for his future house. He did not even look inside the existing 1950s bungalow on the lot before deciding to demolish it completely to make way for this luxurious contemporary structure.

After interviewing ten architectural firms, Duke chose the husband-and-wife team Austin Kelly and Monika Häfelfinger of XTEN. Their proposal showed a strongly horizontal structure designed to require few solid vertical elements so that nothing would interfere with the view. To achieve it, a large ground-floor platform was embedded far into the hillside. The second story, while supported at strategic points, seemingly floats above it. On three sides of both floors, glass walls slide completely open and away into hidden pockets so that nothing stands between Duke and the grand vista. "Normally a building is defined by its facade, which doesn't really exist in this case, so the horizontal lines of the roof and the floors determine the architecture," explains Kelly. Even his colleagues were eluded by his method of holding up the structure, dubbed "Openhouse." In addition to the steel anchored deep in the slope behind the house, the fireplace screen also wraps around and hides massive structural metal beams. The few vertical surfaces—of either oak, concrete, or stone— act as solid, sculptural counterweights to the glass. These were also designed in shades of charcoal to help them recede from the brighter ceilings and floors. Duke opted for a

A reflecting pool that runs the length of the house draws the eye toward the horizon and the view of the city below.

cut pebble flooring material called Sidec to reemphasize the overall effect of bringing the outdoors in. Thanks to wide wraparound decks on both levels, more than half of the 12,000 square feet of total living space sits directly under open skies.

As a fashion designer, Duke thinks constantly about the impact of lines, and is used to burying structurally necessary but visually disruptive seams and darts in the folds of fabric, so it was important to him that his house conceal joints and grooves wherever possible as well. The sensitivity the architects displayed in coordinating the placement of borders between materials to render them unobtrusive impressed him: Kelly and Häfelfinger went as far as aligning door jambs with seams in a mirrored wall, for example. Conversely, Kelly appreciated Duke's exceptional sense of materials and his ability to convey his vision so precisely. The architects did, however, have to adjust to Duke's penchant for last-minute changes—just as he might alter a hem minutes before a runway show, he was equally capable of making sudden changes to building materials. "To try things out at the site was essential, because everything differed greatly from the sketches or models in actual scale and under the real light conditions," Duke says in defense of his methods.

For as strict as he was about the selection of finishes, Duke behaves open-mindedly in choosing the furnishings—everything is given right of entry, from flea-market finds to expensive reclaimed theater seating, and from rustic, crudely hewn tables to Louis XVI–style chairs. These eclectic, mostly light-footed pieces serve as accessories to the more substantial, custom furniture. Sofas capable of seating a dozen people and blocky brass side tables were designed for entertaining a crowd. Shimmery silk pillows and crystal inject a warm gleam into the modern, masculine space. All high-tech objects, such as the huge flat-screen TVs, disappear into built-in cabinetry with the push of a button.

Duke often gives large dinner parties in his garden, where the fragrance of angel trumpet blossoms is omnipresent. Guests assemble at a long table under a beaded chandelier that hangs from a tree branch overhead. On the hill behind the house, he has planted avocado trees, agaves, and succulents—their silvery blue-green has become a favorite color now, one that finds its way into his collections.

OPPOSITE, ABOVE: The house is sited to take full advantage of the 270-degree view.

OPPOSITE, BELOW: At night, the city's glittering lights face competition for attention only from the impressive central fireplace.

With glass walls that slide away completely on both floors, it is easy to see how this structure earned the nickname "Openhouse." The main support beam is cleverly hidden inside the stone fireplace screen.

TOP: Thanks to the steeply sloped site, the bathroom receives unobstructed views of the valley below.

ABOVE, LEFT: A rustic table is surrounded by Louis XVI-style chairs and an ornate bench for visual contrast.

ABOVE, RIGHT: Space beneath a riserless stair fits a baby grand piano perfectly.

OPPOSITE, ABOVE: Mirrored surfaces bring the outdoors deep into the interior. The floor, created from a pebblelike material called Sidec, was used to help create a sense of continuity between outdoor and indoor spaces.

OPPOSITE, BELOW: Dark vertical elements in the bedroom provide a strong contrast to the glass walls.

LEFT: White chaises and outdoor sofas with ample pillows beckon to guests.

RIGHT: A unique orb of a vase perches on the edge of the tub in the master bath.

BELOW: Gardens planted by Duke overlook an intimate outdoor seating area lit by an elegant chandelier suspended from a tree above.

PHILLIP MABERRY AND SCOTT WALKER

# Crazy for Color

Phillip Maberry's earliest memory is of the wallpaper in his parents' bedroom in Dallas—a print of large green and yellow flowers heavily outlined in black. This drastic pattern and the vividly colored 1950s furniture he grew up with infected him with the incurable chromophilia he has passed on to his partner and collaborator in ceramic arts, Scott Walker. The house they have built on the top of a hill in upstate New York is a delirious experiment in color: luminous porcelain bubbles cover a column that rises from the ground floor nearly to the roof, tiles in every shade of the rainbow and in myriad shapes and configurations have overtaken nearly every room in the house. Viewed together, however, the cacophony acts as a neutral, and harmony and order are created out of seeming chaos.

It took the couple a long time to realize their vision for a house full of riotous color. For the first few years that they owned this 40-acre property, they lived in a rickety, rundown log cabin that had been hammered together in the 1960s by people who left Wall Street and had tried, unsuccessfully, to live off the land. Maberry and Walker nicknamed this hippie cottage the Love Shack, because it stood at the end of an overgrown lovers' lane and because of the amount of unrequited love they bestowed on it—for all of their labor-intensive improvements and decorating schemes, they couldn't hide the fact that it was damp, dark, and cold. They would gaze longingly up the nearby hill at what was obviously a more suitable site for a house, and eventually drafted plans for a new three-story structure with double-height windows. They financed the construction with a special limited edition of large plates depicting the original shanty dressed up for each of the four seasons—its appearance in the legendary music video for the song "Love Shack" by the B-52s had generated a cult following. The twelve sets they sold earned the pair enough money to hire a local builder.

Bold color unites a figurative scene and three abstract patterns, all rendered in tile, in the kitchen.

ABOVE, LEFT: Lively curtains created from simple lengths of colored nylon-acetate ribbons were inspired by a similar window treatment at Russel Wright's former home Dragon Rock, which Maberry and Walker rented for a time.

ABOVE, RIGHT: Cheerful colors spill out onto the patio.

OPPOSITE: Breezes activate the multicolored curtain, adding a second layer of visual activity to the already energetic tile floor.

The new house's interior beams—some left visible for their raw beauty—came from hemlock trees growing on the property. Large basalt boulders on the site complicated the floor plan, but the two nature lovers opted to leave them intact. "It would have seemed like an act of violence to blast them away," says Maberry. This decision was inspired by Dragon Rock, Russel Wright's former house in Garrison, New York, which they had rented for three years before moving to the Love Shack, and which similarly features rocky protrusions in the middle of an otherwise strictly rectilinear space.

They incorporated their powerful kiln right into the house as well, but tucked it away behind colored doors that lead to the second-floor studio. It can fire two hundred tiles at a time and has played a crucial role in covering almost every flat surface of the house with an expanse of figurative scenes or vivid abstract ornament. "Tiles are hard, shiny, and extremely durable; their jewel colors will never fade in the sun or darken with age," says Maberry. As a counterpoint to the visual business, many of the walls are painted in subdued hues of yellow or white, and the furnishings are predominantly midcentury modern.

The couple has made it their mission to heal people with what British art critic David Batchelor calls chromophobia—an addiction to anemic beige and gray. He traced the condition's roots to antiquity: Plato denigrated painters as mixers of multicolor drugs, and Aristotle damned colors as intoxicating. According to Maberry and Walker, undiluted doses of red, blue, and yellow will reliably liberate the color-timid of their fears. And for additional confidence they recommend reading Roland Barthes, who called the use of color "a kind of bliss." Their house is living proof.

LEFT: Midcentury modern furniture and a Tulikivi stove imported from Finland share the dining room with one of the basalt boulders around which the house was constructed.

RIGHT: Porcelain bubbles adorn a column that runs the full height of the house.

BELOW: A trompe l'oeil tile rug is one of the bathroom's many exuberant ceramic decorations.

RIGHT AND OPPOSITE: Polka dots and abstract, curved flower motifs on the kitchen counter contrast with rectangular but equally vibrant tiles on the backsplash.

RIGHT: Walls are painted in yellows and whites to provide a calm contrast to the busy patterns elsewhere.

OPPOSITE, ABOVE: Riserless stairs and a unique floor plan allow sunlight to penetrate deep into the interior and activate its many tiled surfaces.

OPPOSITE, BELOW: Cheerful yellow and green pivoting doors separate the tile studio from the main living space.

REBECCA QUAYTMAN AND JEFF PREISS

# Modernism Lives

When this New York couple with a passion for modernist architecture heard that the last of only a handful of houses built by the late artist and architect Tony Smith was for sale, they immediately drove up to Connecticut to see it. All her life, Rebecca Quaytman, a painter who grew up just a few miles away from the site, had heard about a strange and wonderful house on Old Quarry Road. She had always been too shy to stroll into what her family considered an elitist enclave of important midcentury buildings there, and her early attempts to catch a glimpse of the masterpiece from a boat on Long Island Sound had been in vain, so sensitively had Smith—who was trained by Frank Lloyd Wright—integrated it into the landscape. Finally, one fine summer day in 1998, Quaytman received her chance to inspect it up close: she and her husband, cinematographer Jeff Preiss, posed as potential buyers in order to gain entry.

Perched on the highest outcropping of a rare vein of pink granite that surfaces in Canada, briefly again in Guilford, and once more in Africa, Smith's house instantly appealed to them as a work of art, despite the many odd additions that were obscuring its original 1951 plan almost beyond recognition. Still, Smith's striking, intensely sculptural creation of three individual buildings connected by sweeping ramps and porches cast a spell on them. Two weeks after their encounter with the Fred Olsen House—named after the chemical engineer, archaeologist, and avid art collector who had commissioned it—they had to admit to being madly, desperately in love with it.

To consummate their amour fou, Quaytman and Preiss had to overcome many obstacles, the first and most formidable being a previous offer already accepted by one of the three Olsen heirs. The competitors planned to tear down Smith's compound, a crime in the couple's eyes. They rallied support, and in a suspenseful town meeting, an intervention by Terry Riley—from the Museum of Modern Art, where a major Tony Smith retrospective was soon to be mounted—and a rousing speech by architect John Keenen persuaded Old Quarry Association residents to call upon nearly forgotten statutes that allowed for the rejection of prospective buyers by a majority vote, and the unique dwelling was preserved.

The large rock at the center of pool is the focal point around which Tony Smith curved the entire house.

The vision of three sharply geometric shapes arranged radially around a swimming pool occurred to Smith in a dream, "Like a goddess, complete," he wrote. The biggest boulder on the site, which rises out of the saltwater pool, served as the pivotal point of his design. Smith drew concentric circles from it to the edge of the nearby cliff. He then imposed a pentagon on the outermost circle, aligned in relation to the constellations over Long Island Sound, and on these lines he placed the buildings. Fred Olsen had asked Smith to incorporate a large gallery space to house his collection of artworks by Jackson Pollock, Isamu Noguchi, Barnett Newman, Mark Rothko, and Hans Hoffmann. He also requested comfortable guest quarters for these artist friends, but his personal suite of rooms was designed in very modest proportions.

For all their fascination with this architectural masterpiece, its cosmic references and sensitive relationship to nature, the new owners struggled with its eccentricities just as Olsen had, evidenced by his cumbersome additions that sought to make the space more livable. Quaytman and Preiss hired Keenen for a renovation to remove two of Olsen's three additions—which had absolutely infuriated Smith—but kept one as Quaytman's studio. The tiny main house contains the bedroom and an office, while the former gallery with its great north-facing windows has been transformed into a generous living room and kitchen. "But most crucial to making the building practical for everyday use was Keenen's idea to blast a tunnel through the stone to connect our sleeping quarters with the living areas and to create a V-shaped space below," Quaytman explains.

Still, because of the house's open plan, more suitable to warmer locations such as Rio or Los Angeles than the American northeast, the family spends a lot of time in the cold in transit from one building to another. "It's like a little village," comments Preiss. They struggle with the absence of right angles and resulting lack of a certain sense of stability. But they believe this is a small price to pay for the pleasure of living in a magnificent sculpture.

LEFT: Windows in rectangular frames of varying sizes establish a rhythm in the living room.

RIGHT: Midcentury modern furniture, including armchairs in the style of Hans Wegman, at left, complements the house's style and era.

BELOW: Sloped ceilings allow for large, trapezoidal clerestory windows that allow natural light to wash over the original gallery space.

LEFT AND BELOW: Red used as an accent color on simple furnishings throughout the house complements the primary colors found on doors and references the rust-colored cladding outside.

OPPOSITE, ABOVE AND BELOW: Views of the guest house, where the original owner hosted artists including Isamu Noguchi, Jackson Pollock, and Mark Rothko.

ANDRES SERRANO

# Saints and Sinners

The weather outside, the time of day, the building's frosty modern lobby—all are instantly forgotten upon entering this solemn triplex apartment filled with treasures from the Roman empire to the Renaissance. "I wanted to create a nightclub, a church, and a museum at the same time," explains photographer Andres Serrano. The space is populated with religious and mythological figures—resting on a velvet pillow, a carved head of Saint John the Baptist's head greets visitors, and above his desk on the first floor, two iron dragon lamps watch over his business papers.

Serrano's work, which often features religious icons or bodily fluids, sometimes in combination, has been controversial since his infamous *Piss Christ* was exhibited in 1987. It is true that he stopped attending church at thirteen and has rebelled against Puritanism ever since. It is also true that he has conducted photographic experiments involving Ku Klux Klan members and dead bodies in the morgue, and has depicted exotic variations of carnal lust without shame or regret. Anyone can see that this home is deeply influenced by Catholicism, however—its venerated saints as well as its capital sins. The dark splendor of neo-Gothic church furniture, European religious art, and devotional objects from all over the world create an emotionally and spiritually charged space.

This private cathedral knows no ritual, no frankincense, but its every detail speaks of a deep love for the aesthetics of Catholicism, the religion Serrano—the son of an Afro-Cuban mother and a Honduran father—grew up with in Brooklyn. In Serrano's own book of good and evil, though, there is only one unforgivable sacrilege: the creation of something ugly, and in this respect he is utterly innocent. His private residence, like his photography, reveals a strong affinity with Francisco de Goya in emotional depth and fascination with the grotesque, and his fine compositions, lighting, and attention to detail situate both firmly within the realm of art. Just as there is no neutral way of looking at Serrano's work without being overcome with feeling—whether rage, shame, or admiration—it is equally impossible not to succumb to the sacred aura, however tainted, created within his 2,000-square-foot home. Choir stalls and a life-sized statue of Christ, a bishop's chair, and a collection of crucifixes from a Paris flea market, as well as a marble baptismal font create a breathtaking, ecclesiastical atmosphere. Over the years, this fervent collector has delved further and further into the past for items to purchase—he treasures the presence time has bestowed on these remnants of other eras. Serrano wants to be continuously awed and astonished by everything surrounding him, and he expects nothing less from his own works of art.

European religious art and ecclesiastical antiques create an unexpected residential interior.

141

ABOVE: One of Serrano's several human skulls and a blossoming tree branch form a striking memento mori.

RIGHT, TOP AND ABOVE: Antiques from churches, including a life-sized, sixteenth-century statue of Christ, an antique choir stall, and stained glass tucked unexpectedly into a stairwell.

OPPOSITE: A view through Serrano's imposing living room—fitted with a bishop's chair, wrought-iron chandelier, religious statues, and a taxidermized cat—to the more typical West Village neighborhood outside.

LEFT: Drywall covered over with stone forms a thematically appropriate background to Serrano's collection of Renaissance antiques in a guest bedroom.

RIGHT: Sixteen-foot-high ceilings add to the cathedral-like feeling of the space.

BELOW: A Gothic door integrated into the townhouse becomes a uniquely shaped closet entry.

ABOVE: Stone and tile antiques, including a sacrarium converted into a sink and a stone bench with claw feet in the shower bring the religious theme to the bathroom.

RIGHT, TOP AND ABOVE: Every surface of Serrano's apartment has been covered in decorative details, including this tiled archway. An example of Renaissance penmanship and an icon reinforce the mood.

OPPOSITE: The hallway, with its wrought-iron chandelier, religious statue, and carved marble receives an equal distribution of antiques as the rest of the house.

OVERLEAF: Gargoyle doorstops hold open decorative doors to the exquisitely appointed bedroom with its roughly textured brick walls.

# Trouble in Paradise

On this two-acre property near Sagaponack Pond on eastern Long Island, painter, writer, and gardener Robert Dash has one house for the summer—a cool, dark barn hammered together in 1740 from driftwood—and a cottage he occupies during the winter months. Dash prefers the shelter of a weeping willow, however, to either residence, rain or shine, and his enthusiasm for this miniature park known among horticulturalists as an "encyclopedia of garden styles" triumphs over even the meanest weather.

As happy as he may appear standing under its leafy canopies, however, he never thinks of the premises as idyllic. On the contrary. While his true feelings for the garden are revealed by the tender name he has chosen for it—"Madoo," old Scottish for "my dove"—he also views it as a source of unending drama and angst that demands a continuous attention he feels compelled to provide. He has had successes, such as teaching decorative plants and vegetables to coexist peacefully in the same flower bed and training the topiary balls in his gingko grove into immaculate spheres. Still, to Dash the moments of harmony and beauty that result represent only short-lived victories over insects, rabbits, weeds, and the rigors of USDA Plant Hardiness Zone 7a with its salty winds and winter temperatures far below the freezing point, not to mention the occasional hurricanes, which have destroyed dozens of his precious trees.

Madoo began, in 1967, as an outline Dash etched with a tractor borrowed from a nearby farmer into the soil of a potato field, and since then it has developed into a multilayered, elaborate composition. Dash considers both painting and gardening as art forms of the wrist, with the latter the more complex of the two since it involves fragrance, sound, and movement. According to Dash, if Madoo were viewed as a three-dimensional self-portrait, it would reveal someone with an exuberant, generous personality but a tendency toward caprice and recklessness. His hard-earned knowledge has been accumulated painfully over many years by the usual cycle of garden life, death, and plant attrition. His satisfactions, by contrast—as when he admires the perfection of a pretty plant in full bloom—last only a few moments.

Over the years, Dash has added many structures for meditation, like the bridge covered by a pagoda-style roof that overlooks a pond home to countless frogs and water lilies. A rose-lined path designed to create the illusion of depth and a boxwood maze invite visitors to lose themselves in time and place. The gardener rarely indulges in the frivolous pleasure of

Gates and paths dividing the two-acre garden are intended to cause visitors to pause and notice details that might otherwise go unnoticed.

ABOVE, LEFT: Cheerful fresh paint, carefully sculpted hedges and shrubs, and an unusually shaped fountain reveal the care Dash bestows upon the garden.

ABOVE, RIGHT: Formally shaped shrubs coexist peacefully with wilder rhododendrons and trees along a meandering path.

OPPOSITE: An artist's garden, Madoo evolved to incorporate features drawn from many styles and periods, like this bridge with a pagoda-inspired roof.

sitting still, not even in July, when he should reap the fruit of all his labors. He cannot tolerate even the slightest whiff of tiredness among his plants; he feels "morally obliged to eliminate every leaf that displays the first signs of aging." All summer long he plucks, grooms, and waters his plants, severely neglecting his art studio.

By September Dash is looking forward to painting again, and October leaves little time for anything but making jam from wild green grapes. In November he moves into his winter quarters, and with the cold comes silence and loneliness—often his only company is his collection of colorful garden books. By the end of February an irrepressible restlessness corresponding to nature's hidden activities underground rises inside him. All tools have been repaired, oiled, and sharpened, all bushes and trees have been trimmed, and his wicker chairs turned impatiently toward the windows. Dash never longs for the Garden of Eden with what he imagines as its "relentless niceness." He hasn't left Madoo for more than a few hours in years, however, and says each time feels like an expulsion from his very own, if deliciously imperfect, paradise.

LEFT: Dash enlivens the trim of his eighteenth-century shingled studio—a former barn—with bright colors that complement the green of the garden and the blue sky above.

BELOW, LEFT: A long, narrow channel leads to Dash's winter cottage.

BELOW, RIGHT: A lavender gazebo placed among thick vegetation cannot be seen from a distance—it is meant to be a chance discovery for visitors who take the time to wander deep into the garden.

OPPOSITE, ABOVE: Plants of every variety are planted in unusual juxtapositions meant to entice each of the senses.

OPPOSITE, BELOW: Tall, paned windows bring the garden into Dash's studio.

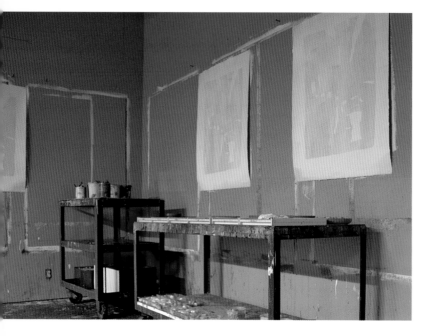

ABOVE AND OPPOSITE: Views
of Dash's studio, where he paints
during the winter months.

FRITZ HAEG

# Taking the Edge Off

Tourists spilling out of buses to admire the architecture of Rudolph Schindler's 1939 Falk Apartments in the Silver Lake section of Los Angeles also inevitably notice and photograph this architecturally intriguing house and its lush yard, full of citrus trees and grapevines, just across the street. The dwelling, created by artist, architect, and activist designer Fritz Haeg, features an elegantly curved concrete garden wall at odds with the house's typical gabled Spanish tile roof. The wall provides the first hint that further unexpected forms await within. From the back, a steep slope falls away to reveal the structure's full three stories and its radical geometry—a 1917 ranch-style wooden core partially enclosed by a curving white shell that relates the house in the spirit of innovation to its modernist neighbor.

Haeg hides most of the original, rustic structure under a simple vertical case but playfully exposes the renovated wooden facade by slicing away two corners of the otherwise rectangular box in graceful arcs. In spite of their smooth contours, these large openings are reminiscent of the holes artist Gordon Matta-Clark cut into condemned buildings in the 1970s. Haeg has mollified Matta-Clark's violent beauty, creating a gentle gesture here—instead of shock there is surprise. The theme of curves and round shapes continues on the interior, evoking feelings of calm and wonder. Upon entering the seemingly modest house, visitors encounter arched doorways, portholes, a vaulted ceiling. All these bent lines combine to take the edge off urban living.

These organic forms and the extensive use of exposed, raw wood for floors, walls, and furniture reflect Haeg's affinity for nature. He even incorporated a piece of jungle right into the center of the house: a former hallway was cut open to the sky to create a sort of terrarium where steady mists produce a perfect climate for orchids and exotic mosses. This miniature rain forest can be viewed through seemingly haphazardly placed round windows that dot the walls of the living room. Another of these punctures is featured on one wall of the media room, an introverted chamber completely clad—like Proust's legendary bedroom—in sound-muffling cork, which still emanates a bitter, tobacco-like fragrance.

Three-story, curved slices on the house's rear facade define its personality and set the expectation for the equally avant-garde interior geometry.

ABOVE, LEFT AND RIGHT: The "conversation pit," a single, curling unit of furniture that seats people in an intimate circle and provides storage for books underneath. An innovative tray is built directly into its surface.

OPPOSITE: Bright paint is used throughout as an inexpensive means of enlivening the rooms. The porthole-like windows at left look into the house's terrarium.

To Haeg nature is not just for decoration or a subject for abstract contemplation, but a source of physical nourishment: every tree and bush he has planted in front and back of the house produces fruits or vegetables. Haeg is also the author of a book entitled *Edible Estates: Attack on the Front Lawn*, a manifesto against America's obsession with immaculate expanses of perfect green blades that depend on chemicals and drain precious water supplies. He promotes the revitalization of the type of individualized, urban agriculture common during World War II and has transformed sterile patches of green into thriving vegetable gardens all over the country. He has also built city habitats for what he calls his "animal clients"— beavers, eagles, and carpenter bees, for example—who he invites to take up residence in the quarters he offers in their former territories, like Manhattan and downtown San Francisco.

The color schemes Haeg employs in the Silver Lake house are also inspired by nature, and reveal the pure joy he finds in it: the dining room glows in a chlorophyll-rich chartreuse, and the living room with its orange hues and west-facing picture window opening onto the famous "Hollywood" sign enhance the spectacular L.A. sunsets. The bedroom on the lower level features deep, sleepy blues. A single compact piece of furniture functions as a bed, closet, nightstand, and chest of drawers. "The goal of all the furniture in the house is to minimize its impact on the room," explains Haeg. The house is arranged and functions with the tightness and efficiency of a boat. While the actual ocean is far beyond the neighboring hills, a large oval pool with black pebbled sides that turns its surface into a mirror gleams at the base of the structure and reflects the house's dramatic geometry.

LEFT: Workaday plywood is elevated to sculptural status when carved into unique, arched forms.

BELOW: In the dining room, the bright vaulted ceiling echoes the curved forms found elsewhere in the house. The built-ins created from the same material as the flooring are a cost-effective and artistic approach to dining furniture.

RIGHT: A wide doorway allows direct access to an outdoor dining patio filled with fruit-bearing trees and edible plants.

LEFT: Textural and insulating cork lines the walls of the cozy media room; a peek into the terrarium is provided by the round window near the door.

BELOW: All bedroom furniture—a storage chest, storage cabinet, nightstands, and even light fixtures are contained in one single built-in unit.

OPPOSITE: Just as each of the other rooms are painted in a single, lively color, the office is splashed with violet. The desk is curved in another iteration of the house's organic theme.

RIGHT: Rosemary bushes along the curved front wall announce Haeg's approach to growing his own food, even in tight urban spaces.

BELOW: Smoothly arcing, organic lines make the house stand out in the Silver Lake neighborhood.

OPPOSITE: A dining set and lamp with rounded, organic forms repeat the lines of the curved facade that opens to provide views of surrounding Silver Lake.

CATHERINE MALANDRINO

# A French Romance on the Hudson River

When this French fashion designer moved to New York City in the late 1990s, curiosity drove her to sample life in several different Manhattan neighborhoods. She settled briefly in apartments from Tribeca to Harlem, even venturing into the very commercial area near the foot of the Empire State Building, and longing for Paris the entire time. On one of her many walks through the metropolis, this dedicated flâneur discovered the Upper West Side, and it offered a cure for her homesick heart. The area's stately, prewar, predominantly Beaux-Arts apartment buildings reminded her pleasantly of Paris's Rive Gauche, and the Hudson proved to be a perfect surrogate for the Seine. Now, at night, she admires the pearllike string of glittering lights on the George Washington Bridge that she can see from her window. "The entire apartment is angled toward this panorama," says Malandrino, who shares the lookout with her husband and business partner, Bernard Aiden, and their son.

As with every apartment she has occupied, Malandrino started out here by introducing bookshelves. The wall-length structure of darkly stained, thick wood holds some of her most important possessions, including several volumes on Oscar Niemeyer—her favorite architect and her son's namesake—and many books by Audubon. There are also silk-covered photo albums in gem tones and souvenirs that spark her imagination, among them the sun-bleached cattle skull Malandrino found on a motorcycle trip through the Arizona desert, whose elegant triangular shape and curved horns later appeared as an abstract pattern in one of her collections. Indeed, Malandrino's fashions are composed much like her interiors: both share combinations of different textures. A high-gloss lacquered floor in the living room contrasts with a zebra skin rug and a pair of shaggy, looped yarn ottomans that she calls her "Rastafarian pets." The juxtaposition of shiny, reflective objects with soft, tactile,

OPPOSITE: Fashion treated as art—including a pair of 1970s platform shoes—is set off by furniture and walls in bright primary colors.

169

RIGHT: Orange accents and a unique mirror perk up a small city bathroom.

OPPOSITE: Simple groupings of like objects decorate the galley kitchen.

often well-worn materials is a constant in her lines and her home. Walls were removed throughout the apartment to maximize light and to accommodate the oversized furniture Malandrino associates with comfort and generosity, such as the giant, lipstick-red sectional sofa.

Fashion is on display everywhere—Malandrino collects 1970s platform shoes too torturous to wear and exhibits them throughout the apartment as sculptures. Vintage purses are scattered decoratively throughout her bedroom, where dresses, skirts, and jackets on a rack create a chic vignette of their own. Even in the living room, zebra-striped boots are playfully paired with a rug of similar pattern on the floor. Her most prized possession hangs above: a 15-foot-long, black-and-white photomural of Manhattan that was originally commissioned for Pennsylvania Station. The nocturnal, luminous image promising exciting, unpredictable adventures that could only happen in New York, her adopted home, serves as the perfect foil to Malandrino's personal realm of serenity and calm.

LEFT: Different textures add visual interest to the living room—shaggy loop-yarn ottomans contrast with the highly lacquered floor, smooth red sofa, and pattern of the zebra rug.

ABOVE: A collection of bowls with graceful forms pop against the room's other colors and add shimmer to the interior.

LEFT: Colorful accessories that pick up on shades in a nearby painting form their own artful vignette.

BELOW: As elsewhere in the apartment, elegant fashion accessories join books and art on display.

RIGHT: Garments from Malandrino's collections share the eye-catching mix of textures found in the apartment's décor.

# Architecture Against Mortality

This cheerful, multicolored facade peeping out of a light-dappled forest of white oak, red acorn, and sycamore trees on a lane in East Hampton, New York, playfully welcomes guests to the abode of artists Shusaku Arakawa and Madeline Gins, but belies the seriousness of each visitor's first moment indoors—which inevitably requires the signing of an insurance waiver. The interior, built over seven years, features a wildly undulating floor of cemented mud shaped into rolling, sand-colored hills with deep valleys and peaks up to 9 feet high that are difficult to navigate for even the most agile.

An instruction sheet handed out to visitors along with this waiver suggests using the tour through the building as a metaphor for touring one's own body and nervous system: Arakawa and Gins consider the rough moonscape a tool for extending the human lifespan by stimu-lating every muscle, all five senses, and the mind. It is a manifestation of the philosophy of Reversible Destiny that they have developed over forty-five years together, the main focus of which is best expressed by the title of the catalog that accompanied their 1997 exhibition at the Guggenheim Museum: *We Have Decided Not to Die*, followed a decade later with an even more provocative book, *Making Dying Illegal*. They believe that comfort is the first step toward ruin, routine the fastest path to the grave, and feel that religions and philoso-phies that assume death is a given poison the world with defeatist thinking.

A former painter who moved to New York from Japan in 1961 with fourteen dollars and Marcel Duchamp's phone number in his pocket, Arakawa is proud of the vivid composition for its blend of science, art, and philosophy. The dramatic "biotopology" forces constant motor concentration, and the palette of forty strong colors that covers the walls, built-in furniture, and floor-to-ceiling poles—placed to provide strategic handholds—is designed to

In place of the usual entry stair, a flow of concrete with the same protuberances found on the interior spills out and down to street level.

jolt the viewer into a state of elevated awareness. To increase the chances for immortality, visual habits and expectations are undermined. Electrical plugs are tilted, window formats and sizes vary, and living areas flow into each other on different levels to demand a constant reexamination of the immediate environment.

The building's eccentric floor plan of four asymmetrical wings houses a bathroom and bedrooms that open onto the central space, without regard for conventional notions of privacy, and is the first instance of a motif found throughout the structure. Its propeller-like shape is repeated in various, unexpected places, like the electronic control board for lights and air conditioning, as the form of a skylight, and in the contours of the kitchen table. There is method, of course, to the seeming randomness of this reappearing pattern: its use in varying scales is meant to cause reflection on different states and sizes of matter, from the atomic to the cosmic. "By moving through this house you will increase your intelligence," claims Arakawa. After a few hours in this challenging environment that only children and pets seem to master with ease, however, some visitors might be glad to discover the alternate exit through the ground-level basement.

ABOVE, LEFT AND RIGHT: The exterior's bright colors were carefully chosen for their ability to engage the senses and keep the mind sharp.

OPPOSITE, ABOVE: Rooms radiate around the kitchen, sunk into the middle of the undulating main floor.

OPPOSITE, BELOW: Vibrant green paint creates a visible—but not physical—barrier between the end of the raised floor surface and the recessed stair leading to the kitchen.

OVERLEAF: Brightly colored poles are placed strategically as handholds for some of the more challenging and steeply sloped portions of the main living space.

LEFT: A recognizably shaped chaise provides some of the only conventional seating, but is rendered in a hard material to discourage the sitter from becoming overly comfortable—and by extension, complacent.

RIGHT AND BELOW: The placement of an oversized, egg-shaped tub in the open bathroom eschews conventional notions of privacy.

HUNT SLONEM

# A Spirited Victorian

"Why should I practice restraint if the world is full of
wonderful things?" asks painter Hunt Slonem, referring
to the opulent interior of his Second Empire–style estate
property in New York's Hudson Valley. "I'm simply not
cut out to be a minimalist." It took him only a few years
to have all thirty rooms of this house, known as Cordts
Mansion after the brick merchant who built it in 1873, restored, painted, and furnished.
Slonem has been collecting mid-nineteenth-century antiques for decades. He loves historical details, especially decorative frills and tassels, as he is the first to admit. All the somber
chairs, sofas, and tables that had been sitting in the raw industrial environment of his city
loft provided him the perfect excuse for purchasing the extravagant country retreat: finally
he could give them a Victorian setting befitting their provenance.

Slonem adopted as his own the four generations of Cordts who lived in the house before him.
Respectfully framed, the photographs of his new ancestors are on display in the parlor. For
Slonem, it is an astonishing experience to live with so much family history that is not his
own—he describes the feeling as a little bit like being a guest in someone else's house. He
does, however, give his own large-scale paintings of his pet toucans, parrots, and cockatoos
that live with him in the city prominent placement as well. His passion for opulent nineteenth-century accessories extends to frames, which he uses for his own canvases. A very
ornate specimen that once held a painting by John Singer Sargent is among his proudest
possessions.

Of the house's original furniture Slonem kept only the dining room set, a special commission
he particularly likes since President William McKinley ate at it once. Often a single object
defines a room's mood for Slonem, and in that case he assembles all other furnishings
around it. The neo-Gothic sofa for example, whose twin is at the Metropolitan Museum,
served as inspiration for everything else in the Black Salon. In the Oriental Room, a small,
nostalgic picture of a graceful temple dancer provided the inspiration for the theme. The
artist describes himself as a city person who never envisioned himself living in the country,
but from the top room in the tower, where Slonem meditates and briefly lets go of all
material things, he can enjoy the river panorama that so seduced the landscape painters
of the Hudson River School before him.

The thirty-room, 1873 Victorian
mansion is sited prominently on
a hilltop that commands sweeping views of the Hudson River.

LEFT: The display of mid-nine-teenth-century antiques side-by-side with Slonem's own art depicting small creatures begins in the formal entry hall.

BELOW, LEFT AND RIGHT: The red parlor's original white, cast-iron mantel cover received an appropriately elaborate decoration of a neo-Gothic clock, candelabrum, and small photos.

RIGHT: Busy original Victorian wallpaper was painted over in solid colors though period-appropriate furnishings in luxurious fabrics were installed.

LEFT AND BELOW: The house's generous proportions give Slonem ample room to display his collections of objects—large and small—gathered over decades.

RIGHT: Colors for each of the rooms were painstakingly chosen—here, a deep yellow and ruby reds are set off by warm light from a multitiered crystal chandelier.

LEFT: In the Black Salon, a series of Slonem's bunnies keep watch over a Gothic settee.

ABOVE: The dining table was the only piece of furniture that came with the house to be retained by Slonem—he personally selected and placed the items in the dozens of other rooms.

LEFT: Inspiration for the Oriental Room came from one portrait of a temple dancer.

BELOW: A casually furnished room tucked away under the mansard roof.

RIGHT: An opulent mirror in the bedroom reveals Slonem's admiration for frames of all sizes. Another of his compositions, placed here for its red background picked up on in the curtains and carpet, is reflected within.

LEFT: Busts, an antique terrarium, and a painting of koi keep diners company in the breakfast room. The pair of chairs are nineteenth-century Eastlake.

RIGHT AND BELOW: Slonem fittingly chose one of his butterfly compositions to hang in a room bursting with plants and flowers.

BENJAMIN NORIEGA-ORTIZ

# Snow White and Pristine

This splendid eighth-floor Chelsea apartment with a view of the nearby Empire State Building is a rhapsody in white—from the blinding snow-white of flawless Greek marble to the soft cirrus-cloud white of Mongolian lamb's fur to the creamy white of the natural wool rug: it would take the vocabulary of an Eskimo to name all the shades of noncolor assembled here by architect and designer Benjamin Noriega-Ortiz. As soon as he and partner Steven Wine walk in, they shed their city clothes immediately and change into a second set of clothing to avoid sullying its pristine surfaces.

The inspiration for this subtle composition came from a string of pearls a friend had given to them as a plaything—it took seven layers of wall paint mixed with mica and marble dust to imitate that same fine, matte shimmer. The lacquer used on the radiators, by contrast, contains glass dust, making for a harder shine. "If you only work with white, different textures are extremely important," explains Noriega-Ortiz. This is not the first time he has experimented with monochrome interiors: his previous apartment on the Hudson was in myriad hues of gray, including that of the battleships he could see from his window. In Chelsea, too, silvery tones form part of his palette: the walls of his foyer are coated in aluminum leaf that bounces cool light around the space, and, next to the lily-white sofa, a cast aluminum reproduction of Frederick Kiesler's famous kidney-shaped nesting coffee table emanates its own icy glow. "The white background is like a stage where each object stands out in the footlights," says Noriega-Ortiz. "Flowers play an important role, and lamps become sculptures."

In order to make the 1,200-square-foot apartment seem more spacious, Noriega-Ortiz not only worked with bright, reflective surfaces—the entire south wall of the living room is mirrored glass—but also with transparency. Noriega-Ortiz finds that looking through one thing to see another creates an impression of lightness and complexity. He opened the windowless bathroom on the lower floor by installing a glass wall that faces the apartment's light-filled north end. When necessary, it can disappear behind a curtain made of a moisture-

A monochromatic approach to the décor highlights the texture of individual elements.

resistant microfiber. On the upper level, he similarly employs a veil of muslin between the kitchen and living room to distance guests from any unsightly culinary messes. Only the windows are devoid of curtains. Here, he decided to support the harsh linearity of the 1970s building, which he works to soften elsewhere. "The architecture pretends to be neutral, but in reality it is very decisive, very defined, very dominant. I counter it with feminine forms and materials," says the Puerto Rican–born designer, adding, "We Latinos are very emotional and tactile." The contrast of using curvy furniture in angular rooms fulfills another purpose as well: from his long experience with Manhattan's boxy apartments, Noriega-Ortiz has learned that avoiding straight lines creates the illusion of a larger room. Instead of conquering the space at a single glance, the eye is forced to wander to fully absorb the arrangement of objects.

This apartment, so functional and cool by daylight, takes on an explicitly sexy personality after sunset. A professional telescope, a gift from Wine's father, sits ready for the rare nights when the stars can compete with the city lights—unfortunately, the instrument came only in black.

ABOVE AND RIGHT, BELOW: Lights designed by Noriega-Ortiz contribute yet another texture to the apartment—feather.

RIGHT, TOP: Sinuous forms on a pair of white chests are enhanced by the stylized leaf borders of the mirrors above them.

OPPOSITE, ABOVE: Even the bed with its sheer, gauzy cover, reinforces the feeling of lightness and texture.

OPPOSITE, BELOW: The striking purity of the apartment's furnishings is highlighted by the view of the city in the background.

PREVIOUS PAGES: The monochromatic decorating scheme creates the illusion that the 1,200-square-foot apartment is larger, and draws attention to the form of individual pieces of furniture. Other pieces, like the slender, transparent desk at right, were designed to retreat quietly into the background.

BARBARA GROSS

# A Courageous Collaboration

All her life, painter, sculptor, and jewelry designer Barbara Gross lived and worked with vivid colors, so simply entering her eighties was no cause to change or retreat into a timid palette of pastels. On the contrary, this glamorous lady chose to radicalize her aesthetic for this home that she calls "her last party." She found a co-conspirator of equal courage and refinement in interior designer Amy Lau. Together, they created a jewel box of an apartment on Central Park. Living room walls of highly polished black Venetian plaster form the ideal background for Gross's abstract paintings and sculptures in shiny metal and smooth stone. Every detail of the interior refers to her art, her travels, her history—allowing her to reflect on a long life well lived.

Once Barbara Gross moved from her house in Great Neck, New York, with the studio loft where she painted and restored furniture for so many years, she embarked on a search for a smaller but comfortable space that would allow her to keep her independent existence. The fact that she carries a rhinestone-encrusted cane custom-made for her by her grand-daughter is an indication that sequestering herself inside a retirement community would not have been an option. Instead, she chose to make herself at home in one of the city's grand Art Deco hotels, the Jumeirah Essex House, which had recently undergone a ninety million dollar renovation that included the creation of fully serviced condominiums. She found the building sparkling enough to represent a fresh start and, most important, it was on Central Park. "When I saw young people kissing under the trees I knew I would never feel lonely here," says the recently widowed artist. Amy Lau positioned a hot-pink chaise longue right at the picture window—a front row seat for this benevolent voyeur.

A metallic sideboard edged in aqua picks up the shimmer of the art above, the glass-and-chrome side table, and the arm-chair's curved back.

Only a small selection of objects from Gross's previous life could fit into the two-bedroom space, but she and Amy Lau found innovative ways to express her personality nevertheless. Lau took most of her clues from the art: "Barbara has a strong interest in metallurgy, even her paintings contain metal, and that's how I started my own alchemical process— echoing their cool shimmer with silk, chrome, glass, with metal threads in the bedroom curtains, and mother of pearl in the bathroom walls," she explains. Gross also provided plenty of ideas of her own, such as determining that a pair of velour-covered, barrel-back chairs would be better upholstered in unexpected black patent leather. A pattern from one of her abstract paintings was also repeated verbatim in a silk rug. Lau discovered a collection of Emilio Pucci skirts from the 1970s in Gross's closet and turned the colorful velvet textiles into pillow covers that complement the apartment's style perfectly. The entire space is tailored to fit her in every way.

ABOVE, LEFT: Square-bodied dining chairs on metallic legs were inspired by Gross's sculpture on the far wall.

ABOVE, RIGHT: The apartment's edgy black-plus-metallic theme begins in the entry hall.

OPPOSITE: Pillows made from Gross's Pucci skirts complement the pink chaise from which she overlooks Central Park.

OVERLEAF: Bold colors, black Venetian plaster walls, and strong patterns attest to the owner's daring personality.

LEFT AND RIGHT: Wallpaper gets an unexpectedly avant-garde treatment in a guest bedroom.

BELOW: Patterns and colors from Gross's art were replicated in the custom silk rug.

WILL BARNET

# A Living Tradition

Most evenings, the National Arts Club in Manhattan receives elegantly dressed guests who make their way through a white marble foyer filled with an imposing row of bronze busts, enter a room filled with soft Victorian twilight cast by John La Farge's stained-glass ceiling, and dine in the company of like-minded friends of the arts. The historic Tilden Mansion has housed this venerable institution for more than a hundred years, along with a few dozen highly coveted apartments cum studios reserved for artists.

Since 1982 painter Will Barnet and his wife Elena, a former dancer, have been privileged to occupy a duplex here that features a 9-foot atelier window overlooking Gramercy Park. The neighborhood had fallen into relative obscurity when Barnet's friend Everett Raymond Kinstler, a long-time artist in residence who painted numerous portraits of U.S. presidents and other luminaries that now adorn the club's walls, suggested that he should apply for an apartment himself. Applicants are required to donate a major work to the National Arts Club collection—which contains pieces by George Bellows, William Merritt Chase, and Charles Hawthorne, among many others—and be approved by an infamously strict selection committee. With a career that began shortly after World War I and that has produced countless drawings, prints, and paintings, and due to his half-century tenure as a teacher at the Art Students League, Barnet proved eligible.

Art supplies and figurative paintings take up most of the tall space that is the center of the couple's life. We see his older sisters, two milliners who never left their hometown of Beverly in New England and have lived together all their lives. His father's pet parrot appears in several works, as does Madame Butterfly, a beloved cat who was a very patient model. A tender *mise en abîme* is created when Gramercy Park serves as the backdrop to a portrait of his daughter jumping from one of its benches as a child. The influence on his art from his former employment as a lithographer during the Great Depression, when he first arrived in New York, is clear. He took emotional refuge from the terrible social conditions he witnessed around him during that time by frequenting the city's museums, and then by confronting them in his own work as well. Over the past few decades, however, Barnet has returned to his favorite subject—the playful relationship between people and animals. When the atmosphere filled with these memories on the quiet eighth floor seems too still, the Barnets need only take the elevator downstairs to meet up with kindred spirits in the salon who are always keen for conversation about art.

A broad staircase in the entrance of the National Arts Club leads to the main reception rooms.

RIGHT AND BELOW: Creative
clutter of the highest order
attests to Barnet's ongoing
devotion to his art.

OPPOSITE: A tall window floods
the studio with prized north
light from Gramercy Park.

LEFT: A long rectangular canvas of Barnet's hangs in the living room.

BELOW, LEFT: A regular motif in Barnet's work, the crow, appears in this work clearly influenced by his time as a lithographer.

BELOW, RIGHT: Art given to Barnet by friends and former students is lovingly hung in the kitchen.

OPPOSITE: Eclectic art gathered in the living room—an African sculpture on the mantle, a portrait in oil, and a wrought-iron candelabrum—reveals the presence of an owner with wide-ranging artistic interests.

A straightforward plaque and
an abstract copper sculpture
announce the entry to Barnet's
apartment and studio in this
institutional hall that belies
the charm of the apartment
beyond.

CHRISTOPHER BORTUGNO

# Master of All He Surveys

The abandoned, vine-covered original farmhouse on the 400-acre dairy farm in Kinderhook, New York, where Christopher Bortugno grew up had always intrigued him—his father, on the other hand, considered it an eyesore but never got around to tearing it down. After standing vacant through the 1970s, the ceilings caved in, the plaster walls crumbled, and part of the stairwell collapsed. A sumac took root in the basement and raised its scrawny branches through the broken windows. As a teenager Bortugno spent many nights roaming the empty house, running his flashlight over the rubble—the decaying 200-year-old brick walls, the broken marble fireplace, and the creaky wooden floors. He dreamed about restoring it to its former splendor. "People said the house was haunted," he said. "I always saw it as something precious, something that could shine and sparkle."

Today that Dutch Colonial house is Bortugno's home, a place of unlikely elegance that has largely returned to its original 1810 condition, but with some interventions. He tore out the decrepit central staircase, which impeded progress through the front door, and moved the steps to the side of the entrance instead, immediately improving the flow and making the space more welcoming. Original walls that partitioned the ground floor into five rooms were eliminated in order to create one large, open area. "I wanted to preserve as much as possible of its historical beauty; however, I prefer an open space to a cluster of tiny rooms," he explains. The kitchen was banished to the basement so his vision for a dining area free from the disturbance of banal-looking appliances could be achieved. He even took out the attic floor, creating a cathedral ceiling under the gambrel roof.

Moving the position of the staircase to create a wider, more welcoming entry was one of Bortugno's first renovations to the house. His front door, literally as well as figuratively, is always open to friends.

From these heights Bortugno hung a brass chandelier—a highborn object down on its luck that he had found languishing among other outcasts in a thrift store near Hudson, New York. He remolded the graceful curves of its long crooked arms and crowned it with a brass pineapple scavenged from a yard sale. The pineapple, a symbol of hospitality, is a fitting detail for a house where the door is never locked. Friends and neighbors drop in regardless of whether Bortugno is out working or not—even his billy goat is allowed to wander into the living room.

Bortugno's profession means thirteen-hour workdays that begin at five in the morning with milking 120 cows, then maintaining silos, working in the fields, feeding the animals, veterinarian visits, and milking sessions again in the early evening, so the house restoration was by necessity a largely nocturnal activity. Repairs and installations of found objects happen in the middle of the night. Decorating came naturally to him, he says, but he also learned a lot from an old friend, the late fashion photographer Jack Clark, who left him a mahogany buffet from the 1820s and a cherry wood dining table. These elegant antiques now gracefully cohabit with the treasures Bortugno has foraged from sundry other places. Farm life itself has played an important role in Bortugno's ability to transform a dilapidated building into a very personal one. "You acquire a lot of practical skills," he explains. "But most of all you learn to work with what you have."

ABOVE: Bortugno carefully refinished surfaces by hand, including the walls and floor-boards.

RIGHT: A nine-dollar chandelier found at a local Hudson, New York antique dealer appealed to Bortugno for its pineapple-shaped motif: a traditional symbol of hospitality.

LEFT, RIGHT, AND BELOW:
Bortugno removed part of the
second floor to create a lightwell
that reaches from the basement
to the roof, exposing the underside of the classic Dutch Colonial
roof and creating a niche for his
piano in the process.

LEFT: Bricks in the basement were placed when the house was first constructed, nearly 200 years ago.

BELOW, LEFT AND RIGHT: Copper pots gathered at various garage sales form the bulk of Bortugno's cooking implements.

OPPOSITE: The kitchen was relegated to the basement in order to devote more first-floor space to entertaining.

BRIDGET VAGEDES AND TIMOTHY KREHBIEL

# Freedom High Above Los Angeles

The search for more studio space for her booming business, Artafacts, led this jewelry designer from Venice Beach all the way to an industrial section of downtown Los Angeles. The contrast between the oceanside enclave with its romantic canals and this neighborhood of warehouses, factories, and artists' lofts, as well as a large homeless population, couldn't have been sharper, but Bridget Vagedes and her husband Timothy Krehbiel, an architect and restorer of 1950s woodie cars, were intrigued when they stumbled upon a strange freestanding corner property: a 120-foot-long building shaped like a piece of a cake and completely covered with a thick icing of concrete—an emergency measure taken by the owners to keep parts of the the crumbling facade intact and to keep vandals out. Inside this bunker, utter silence and the deepest darkness reigned, with no electricity available to dispel it. When the adventurous couple entered the forgotten building armed with flashlights and counted sixteen boarded-up windows, each over 5 feet high, they decided to buy it.

Even once they had removed the 4-inch-thick concrete cocoon and installed plumbing and electricity, however, they didn't move into their 6,000-square-foot, two-story structure, but on top of it—into a tiny 1950s Zenith camper which they'd hoisted onto the roof, to be precise. The couple had begun working in the warehouse after its renovation, but were still living in Venice and the commute each way was normally over an hour, leading Vagedes to choose to simply pull her Cadillac into the garage and sleep in its back seat after long days more and more often. Their initial solution was to park the aluminum trailer—which had been languishing in a Long Beach parking lot until Krehbiel bought it for next to nothing—behind the warehouse. He planned to use it to take his wife on a ride to Baja, Mexico, but the 5,212-pound caravan took off for its last foreseeable journey to the L.A. rooftop instead. He had it hoisted up by crane, and Vagedes found it there, adorned with holiday lights and a big red bow, when she returned from a business trip to Indonesia in December 2003. "Living up here, I feel a world away—nobody even knows you're there, but you can observe everything that is happening down in the streets," she says. For a practiced nomad who had roamed the world over, from Italy to Russia and Taiwan, living in a mobile structure somehow seemed fitting.

A view of the 5,000-pound, 200-square-foot, 1959 Zenith camper on the roof.

The couple loves falling asleep under the open night sky and waking up to the sounds of workmen hammering to the beat of Mexican music below. They watch hummingbirds who have found the way through the treeless industrial territory to their potted bougainvillea bushes and baby palm trees surrounding their silver caravan. Such breezy freedom is made possible by the vast space allotted to storage below: the ground floor now looks like a small theater company's prop shop, with objects from Chinese lanterns to 1950s TV sets stored there. Several coat racks hold Vagedes's collection of over three hundred vintage dresses and sequined roller-skating outfits. Upstairs in the jewelry atelier, however, orderliness rules. Hundreds of glass jars containing chain links and Murano glass beads sit on steel shelves as in an extremely organized laboratory. It is here that the extent of the couple's careful restoration is most apparent—sanded brick walls, exposed steel ceiling beams, arched windows, and polished wooden floors give the space a professional calm.

Since the minute, 200-square-foot capsule on the roof doesn't provide any room for furniture—everything is built in—Vagedes's interior design ambitions had to be satisfied by making curtains, finding small flea-market decorations, and hanging a chain of flamingo lights. But there are many more items on the wish list: a trapeze for Vagedes, who likes to perform acrobatic acts; an indoor swimming pool; and a vintage greenhouse for the roof that could become her personal bathroom. "All these are doable dreams," Vagedes claims. She is in no rush to realize them, though—she really likes to improvise.

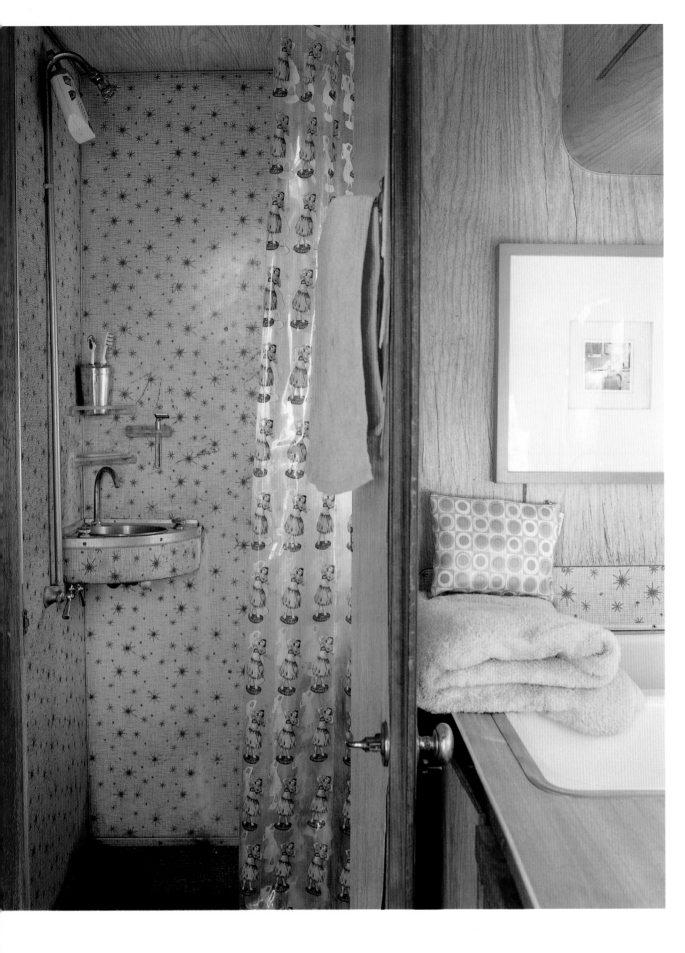

LEFT: The Zenith's minuscule bathroom, enlivened by a vintage starburst linoleum, is quaint but the couple's main complaint with living on the roof—a lack of water pressure means showers run out after just five minutes.

OPPOSITE, ABOVE AND BELOW: Built-in furniture meant Vagedes had to channel her interior design energies in two narrow directions—curtains and flamingos.

LEFT: A vintage woodie station wagon awaiting Krehbiel's attention.

BELOW: An upright piano becomes the base for a carefully arranged display of personal memetos.

RIGHT: The spacious jewelry studio allows Vagedes to keep her materials arranged in organized rows of jars and bottles.

LEFT AND ABOVE: Vagedes's small rooftop flower garden takes the place of a traditional yard.

Thanks to all the people who helped me with this project.

I would also like to thank my friend Uta Winkler for her unwavering support and her unfailing taste.


—Bärbel Miebach